The Book of Number

Practical Workbook

The complete workbook for the practical application of Pythagorean Numerology

By Michael Wallace (Raven)

The Author wishes to thank and offer gratitude to the following for their assistance.

Primarily, the writers of the Pythagorean tradition, but in particular Guthrie, whose "Pythagorean Sourcebook" (Phanes Press) provides an amazing insight into how the Pythagoreans thought.

It goes without saying that the efforts over generations by those in our universities, as well as organizations such as the Rosicrucian and Theosophical Society, to preserve the knowledge of antiquity is what makes books like this possible.

The writing of Paul Twitchell in the late 1960's also provided me with valuable insights to the Spiritual Aspect of Number, and an appreciation of how the individual can travel to inner worlds to discover truth directly.

Also, for those who choose to accept the concept of life after death, the visits from Pythagoras in the dream state gave me the clues and direction to get past every obstacle that came my way in the recording of this knowledge.

I extend warm thanks to my father for the extensive corrections and proof reading, but also for the fascinating books he had on his shelf that started my interest in arcane wisdom.

Finally to Ross Chamings for his ongoing support and insight, as well as his beautiful photographic cover art. It must be noted that these photos are not digital creations, but actual photos of real world objects in macro lens.

It is better wither to be silent, or to say things of more value than silence? Sooner throw a pearl at hazard than an idle or useless word; and do not say a little in many words, but a great deal in a few.

Pythagoras

Other Books by the author:

Jermimiah Versus the Grabblesnatch

The Divinity Dice Series

Ratology: Way of the Un-Dammed

Hello Planet Earth

Welcome to the Book of Number

The Pythagoreans held that number was the language the Gods used to speak with man. The Noumenon was the great unformed divine power that broke into phenomenon as it entered into the worlds of matter, space, energy and time. Creation had a number, and Numerology was the way to understand this.

It is some 35 years since I first encountered the concept of Number being used as a tool for spiritual truth and personal growth. In that time I have studied many books, and travelled the world looking at sacred sites. As I researched the ancient history of divination, it always fascinated me how a simple set of Numbers could say so much, and in such accurate detail, about a person I didn't know.

It is a principle of Numerology that specific patterns of number have specific meanings. Numerology expands numerical data found in such areas as your date of birth, and defines the patterns found there into things called Aspects. Each individual Aspect has a specific meaning. Based on your personal numerical information, a Numerologist will go over these aspects and form them into an interpretation that is relevant to the individual.

Every individual has a variety of these Aspects at work in their life, and they are not particularly difficult to find and record. However, understanding how they all mesh is not so easy. Each individual is a puzzle box the Numerologist must solve.

2500 Years of History

This started with Pythagoras over 2500 years ago. The man himself did not invent Numerology, he simply organised it and made it functional. What he did was resolve and re-map the complex notions and complicated techniques of the ancients into a more obvious and understandable structure.

Of course, Numerology is but one of the things he distilled. The Pythagoreans explored geometry, trigonometry, mathematics and philosophy, but in all there was one constant. Everything was subject to the principles of logic and reduction to the obvious.

And so it is with this book you now hold. It has taken enormous research and many years to compile and condense this work into the essence of Pythagorean Numerology.

The journey of this book started in 1991 with the birth of my youngest son. I was perplexed with the lack of a cohesive study on Pythagorean Numerology, and just started writing down what I found had worked. Before and since that date I had read and studied most forms of Numerology available in the world today. I found the core Pythagorean principles of Logic, Simplicity and Clarity to be in short supply in most of what I researched.

Numerology relies on simple, clear logic. A good Pythagorean Numerologist is able to take any complex issue a person is suffering from, and convert it to an understanding, that is both obvious and clear, that this soul can work with.

Once you understand the basics in this book you too will be able to see the patterns at work in someone's life. What is more, you will learn to do this quickly, and easily. Given a few numerical facts, you will be able to expand anyone's numerical chart into an understanding of the individuals concerns in mere minutes.

It is Fast, it is Simple, it is Accurate.

Of course, seeing a pattern is one thing. Understanding what it means requires a degree of wisdom, but working out the patterns of itself is a mechanical process that anyone can learn.

I have attempted to keep things clear and uncluttered, but there are a lot of small details to move through. A good deal of focus on your part will be required. However, it is worth it. I know it works because I have thousands of case histories behind me. Many times I have never met the people, yet they write to say they were staggered at how much I appeared to know about them, and how clear the solutions to their questions were.

It takes time to learn the language of Number, and to grasp all the fine points, but if you apply yourself, inside a mere few weeks you will be able to work out a chart, and amaze your friends with the extraordinary accuracy of the Pythagorean method.

The journey starts right now.

Course Guidelines

On the opposite page is the original course structure. The client psychology has been separated from the practical course, but it is recommended you keep to the basic course structure. The original intent was to learn one core aspect of the practical application, and at the same time contemplate the inner workings of understanding how clients think and feel.

If you get lost in all the details, come back to this page and refocus on the overview.

ORIGINAL COURSE GUIDELINES

Understanding the Client: Psychology of Clients
Client Profiling: ID Quotient
Understanding the Primary Birth Number: Fadic Numbers

Understanding the Client: The Elements
Resolving Primary Numbers: Dominant and Composite Numbers

Understanding the Client: The Four Querent Types
First level of the Chart: Noumenal Flow Chart

Understanding the Client: The Survival Scale
Cycles: A brief Study of CYCLES

Understanding the Client: MEDIA
Studies of the Matrix: General introduction

Understanding the Client: The Censor
Understanding Number Weight: NOUMENAL WEIGHT
Studies of the Matrix: Lines in the Matrix

A study of the basic Laws: Laws and Principles
Studies of the Matrix: Trines in the Matrix
Interpretations of Lines in the Matrix: (Link from: Trines in the Matrix)

The Purpose of Virtue: Knowledge is Not Virtue
Studies of the Matrix: ADVANCED: Patterns in the Matrix

A Study of Spiritual Harmonics: HARMONICS
Studies of the Matrix: ADVANCED: The Overlay Matrix

Further Harmonic Studies: Numero Ordo Selectorum
Important Variations in the Matrix: DOUBLETS
Added Items of Note: Symbols. Letters and their Meanings.

A Study in the Psychology of Choice: Vases at the Portal
Closing Comments: Harmonic Principles

The Book of Number: Practical Workbook

Copyright © 2014 Michael Wallace

All Rights Reserved

This book is published under the Berne Convention. All copyright protected to the author. No prior use without permission except for excerpts for review or educational purposes. All enquiries via Email to: info.numberharmonics@gmail.com

Published by Ladder to the Moon Publications.
ISBN: 978-0-9756994-4-7
Mailing: PO Box 1355 Kingscliff, NSW 2487
WEB: www.bookofnumber.com.au
All rights reserved to the copyright holder.

INDEX

Welcome to the Book of Number	4
From the Noumena to Phenomena	10
Introduction	11
Numerology Master Class	20
Sacred Principles of Simple Addition	34
Dominant and Composite Numbers	35
Noumenal Flow Chart	43
Noumenal Flow Chart - Blank Chart	52
Cycles	53
Matrix Studies	65
Noumenal Weight in the Matrix	80
Lines in the Matrix	86
Trines in the Matrix	96
Pictorial Summary of Trines	103
Patterns in the Matrix	109
Pictorial Summary of Patterns	111
The Overlay Matrix	117
Doublets and Magic Squares	127
Symbology	136
Letters and their Meanings	143
Harmonic Balance	146
Epilogue	150

From the Noumena to Phenomena

The Noumenon is the vast, unstructured presence that contains within it all potential, all possibilities, and all dimensions of existence. The Noumena, which is the individualized energy from Noumenon, moves into the Matter, Energy, Space and Time universe, and becomes the physical reality we term Phenomena.

It's a little like how we have "The Cloud" on the web from which everyone can draw down information.

The Pythagoreans held that this process of creation is described by the numbers that occur in a person's life. If there is a "One" in a person's chart, it is connected in some way to the spiritual essence of One, that which emanated from the Noumenon. They held that all life is connected in a seamless series of Numbers, which you could analyse if you understood the pattern.

Just as a musician can read a chart that has black dots on lines, and from it produce beautiful music, so too can a Numerologist look at the Number Chart of an individual, and draw from it extraordinary truths.

Pythagoras said, "We are a song". You are a song, but can you hear yourself singing?

This book is the first in centuries to contain all the basic elements of the Pythagorean Teaching of Number. It has taken some 23 years to construct from the "cloud" of the the past. Everything here has been tested, and proven by the author in real life situations.

May your journey here be fruitful.

INTRODUCTION

The Great Order of Number

Divination has been a constant with all human civilization. There is not one single culture where people have not tried to understand what might be coming in future events, or sought, in some way, to understand the will of the Gods. The word religion is based on the Latin root, "religare". It means "to re-tie" or reconnect, and divination, in its many various forms, is really seeking to understand, to reconnect, with the divine will.

Divination is the one thing that differentiates us from nature. While the opposable thumb, the creation of tools, and the powerful motivation of self-interest were driving forces in what created civilization, behind all this we carry an urge other animals simply do not possess. Humans, unlike the other apes, like to know what's around the bend. Why? For one, it gives us a competitive edge.

If a farmer growing crops can get some idea when the rains would come, he knows the best time to plant his seed. This gives him a competitive advantage over his neighbour. If the hunter could go to someone with "second sight" who could tell him where he could find the antelope, this would give him an advantage.

The Art of Divination grew out of these simple beginnings. The high point came in Ancient Greece, where Delphi, and the Oracles in general, became the spiritual consulting room for our civilization. No king went to war without first consulting an oracle, and if they could afford it, a rich man saw an Oracle before any new venture.

Originally the various types divinations were developed in an attempt to understand the Will of the Gods. The throwing of bones, casting of dice, and reading the stars are all part of a shared human history, one of seeking to understand the divine plan.

And one of the earliest forms of divination is Numerology.

NUMBER is congruent with the development of civilization.

Logically, it stands to reason that the study of number could only come about after someone had something to count. People had to HAVE stuff in order to want to count it, yes? Obviously, if you want to raise taxes, build bridges and do all the things you need to do to have a civilization, numbers and mathematics are essential. Our entire culture is based on the forces of Language and Number.

The Pythagoreans held that life spoke to us directly, and through analysing number patterns, you could hear it's voice. It is a language we can learn. If you do, you will see in absolute clarity how life is talking to you through everyday events via numerals.

HAKATA: Shona Dice

Divination using Number comes from several known sources. Most ancient of all are the casting of flat "dice" used by early African tribes. Early forms of number divination were developed from the types of dice (pictured) that are currently used by the Shona. But it appears that the first formal system of Numerology occurred in India, in or around 4000 BC. In a similar time frame we find Chaldean Numerology, which is said to come from Kabala.

The I-Ching is Chinese Numerology. It was formally structured as "The Book of Changes" in or around 1000 BC, but its actual history is far older and the origins are unknown.

So, where did Pythagorean Numerology come from?

Pythagoras studied for 23 years in the Egyptian Mystery Schools (a rare honour). At this time Cambyses and his Persian army conquered Egypt, and Pythagoras was taken back to Babylon. He studied there for 12 years, and in the process amalgamated the Chaldean (Egyptian) and Vedic forms of number analysis. He appears to have created his own system of Number Divination.

More specifically, he amalgamated the complex numerical system of Egypt with the decimal system of India, and introduced this to Ancient Greece. Pythagoras incorporated the Greek mathematics he had learned from Thales (his original teacher who sent him to Egypt) and Vedic Math to create the basis of modern Math. His return to Croton effectively started the Golden Age of Greece. He introduced Trigonometry, Geometry, and Philosophy. He also developed the spiritual analysis of number we call Numerology.

To the Greeks of 500 BC, the spiritual aspects of Number were aligned to the mundane practical aspects. In the ancient Greek way of looking at things, the mathematics that allowed you to calculate the stones needed to build a bridge also contained the spiritual nature of the object created. The external reality and internal truth were seen as connected via the spiritual force known as the "E" or the Ekstasis. (Where the verb ecstasy comes from)

Numbers themselves were seen as a form of Divinity. If you truly understood the nature of Number, you understood the Nature of the Gods. Sadly, the path from the Golden Age of Greece, through the Dark Ages and Middle Ages to the present, has robbed us of the spiritual quality of Number. Yet, even in the empty shell left behind, we can still hear the oceans of antiquity, whispering.

The ancient world was known for it's oracles and haurispices (Estruscan diviners). No important action was taken by a country unless some seer or diviner was first consulted. Oracular Divination was seen as an essential aspect in the normal course of planning or the future. Of course, it became corrupted and fell into disrepute.

Christianity brought an end to the era of Oracles. After 692 AD, the Council of Trullo (under Justinian the Second) banned all forms of divination. Yet the study of Number, necessary for the construction of buildings and calculation of taxes, was exempt. So it survived. Many will attest that the Bible, itself, is written in a numerical code.

While the divine nature of Number was no longer encouraged or taught, echoes of the ancient ways came to our present day with the discovery in Rome (1993) of a Temple to Pythagoras. It appears to have been shut down and sealed at the time that is congruent with the Council of Trullo.

At this point in history, in the Roman world, all forms of pagan worship were disavowed, yet the teachings and the mathematics of Pythagoras were still permitted. Even so, while the man's legacy has survived, the sense of connectedness the Pythagoreans achieved has been fragmented. The pieces were all still there, but the jigsaw had become scattered and confused.

This is why, in 1991, I set about rectifying the situation regarding Numerology. This book you now hold came about directly from my personal frustration at finding any single resource that adequately contained the genuine Pythagorean Method. After some 20 years of personal experience reading number charts and digesting just about everything available in the field of Number Study, I could find not one single, authoritative source that related directly to the Pythagorean Tradition.

There were many variations of Number Divination: Gematria (Masonic Numerology), Chaldean, Cabalist, Jaffar, and forms of Pythagorean numerology, and there were some (like Godwin) who seemed to reinvent the wheel almost entirely.

In the modern cycle, Cheiro's Book of Number is the most striking reawakening of this ancient art. However, in 1903 a publication, "The Mysteries of Sound and Number" by S H Ahmad came during the Spiritual Renaissance triggered by Madam Blavatsky and the Spiritualist movement. This book, apparently derived from Sufi Traditions, created a good deal of interest in Numerology, most likely because it promised a way to win money with horse racing!

There have been many other books and writings in a similar vein.

I do not disparage any of these. After all, there are four systems of Western Astrology that all seem to work for the practitioners of same, as well as Chinese, Indian and Egyptian Astrology.

No single person or system can contain the "all" of existence. That said, the original teachings of the Pythagoreans had something the others did not: simplicity. The original teachings also have a mathematical background along with a comprehensive grasp of patterns and the natural order. It is simply better, and quicker.

This is the key to all things Pythagorean: The teachings are about ESSENCE and PURITY. I have found this true in all that relates to the Pythagorean Principles. Thus we find there is a core simplicity at the heart of Pythagorean Number Interpretation. This is as true with their practice of Music Healing, as it is with the elegant simplicity of the Pythagorean Theorem we all studied at school.

PYTHAGORAS

Here we need to stop and understand just what Pythagoras did. There are very clear reasons why he continues to be held up as one of the great spiritual, and practical, masters in all of history.

People say he invented Trigonometry, Geometry, the Decimal System, etc. but this is not correct. What Pythagoras did was to take ancient wisdom, and REFORM it. He reshaped the old truths that were locked away in the guilds, and transformed these into transmutable teachings than anyone with intelligence and sufficient application could master.

Many overlook his most important contribution, the UNIVERSITY. Before Pythagoras, you had to be apprenticed to a master, and usually you would then be locked to the practice of that trade your entire life. He changed all of this. He created a place where ANYONE (including women) could go to learn. He created a world where a person could choose their destiny through education.

We have all heard of the Pythagorean Theorem. This study of the right angle triangle had been long known to the Egyptian rope stretchers, (our original geometric engineers) and others, but it was treated as a "trade secret". The Theorem that bears his name is a perfect example of what Pythagoras did. He "invented" nothing, he just described this principle in a way that anyone could understand.

He reformed ancient wisdom and truth, and put it in a shape that could be easily taught. So now, anyone could become a mason, or a carpenter. Pythagoras set the knowledge free, and reorganised it so it was accessible to all.

Ideally, this is what the book you are currently holding will do for you. My sole aim is to set free the ancient teachings in a way that you can understand, and in a format you can use.

Obviously, there are many details to grasp. There are many layers to the cake, and many specific things to learn, but as you go step by step through the process, in short order you will come to the point of understanding how it all works as a cohesive whole.

The Sacred Principle of Twelve

This is absolutely core to the entire study of Number. Twelve numbers form the basis of what there is to know in Pythagorean Numerology. There are only Twelve points of reference to learn.

Twelve numbers represent Twelve doors to the deepest spiritual truths. These relate directly to the Twelve notes of music. By grasping the truths inherent in each, you will learn to grasp how they combine to make the whole. It is like a language with just Twelve letters, one that you can get a hold of, and learn to speak, with relative ease.

That is what I liked about Numerology. My father is an astrologer, and while the incredibly complex and convoluted layers can add up to insights of remarkable clarity, it takes years to grasp the basics. With the study of Number, you can get it in weeks. I LIKE this.

You can be reading this book today, and by following the steps described, within days you can be doing readings for friends.

Just as Pythagoras cut away the dross and padding that clouded the ancient paths, and reduced everything (like the study of number) into a simple, clear teaching anyone could grasp, I do the same for you. So, we come to the present day and the book you currently hold, and a few terms you may not understand.

As you read through this, what you actually hold are thousands of years of observations condensed into English. In truth, no book can give you the secrets of the Noumenal (Spiritual Number) Order. This publication is both your introduction and your invitation to step into the doorway each number represents. Perhaps you may even walk through this door to the inner worlds where it comes from.

Which brings us to the reason we are here, to help you become a practitioner of Numerology: a Numerologist.

As a Numerologist, your goal is to see the chart before you in much the same way as another person reads a book. As you open up a chart, it is like a picture forming in a frame. As you understand the patterns before you, they take shape and crystallise to a clear image. Then you walk into the picture represented by the chart you are given, and bring it to life inside your mind and heart.

This is what I do. If you can learn to do this, you will discover each person's chart is alive and vibrant, full of potential and possibility.

But first, we need to grasp the basics. In the original form, this book was a correspondence course called "The Magic of Number" and this was sent as a monthly mail-out, with a spiritual dialogue in front of each section of the practical aspects of doing a reading.

However, for the purpose of this study book I have recompiled all of the original course into four separate compartments. Two actual books you can buy, and two books in download form

1. **Practical Application:** The physical things to learn that allow you to compile a chart from someone's birth date, etc.
2. **Book of Interpretations:** Obviously, the book holding the interpretations. It is the companion to the course proper. For those who qualify, (there is a test) this can downloaded. You can then cut and paste the interpretation, thus making the compiling of a chart much easier.
3. **Spiritual Principles:** The psychological and spiritual focus required to become a successful reader. (Download Dialogue)

4. **On-Line Chart Examples:** These are actual charts you can refer to online to help you get an overall focus on how the process works.

I also include the original course guidelines (immediately prior to this Introduction) that allow you to work with the structure of the 1991 correspondence course, if you so choose.

In closing this introduction, I want to first welcome you, and second to warn you. There is a great power still active in these teachings, and should you delve deeply into them, your life will change.

Whether you believe in Past Lives (transmigration of Soul was a core teaching with the Pythagoreans) or not, as you study the truth of Number, energies from the distant past may stir and become active in your life.

As you break through to new understanding, you will be shattering old patterns inside yourself, and alternating tides of circumstance will begin to flow. So, if you like your life as it is, if you do not want change, do not start this book.

Learning the practical aspects is one thing, but when you start to practice and apply this knowledge on friends and relatives, you will awaken the ancient, dormant forces within you. In doing so the new forces will activate inside yourself, and flow outwards. This WILL change your circumstances and your relationships with others.

This is the nature of Spiritual Truth. As you enter into IT, IT enters into YOU. The net result is change for the better, but this often involves the dismantling of conditions and habits of the past.

I wish you well on the journey.

Michael Wallace (Raven)

Gold Coast, Australia, June 2013

"most men and women, by birth or nature, lack the means to advance in wealth or power, but all have the ability to advance in knowledge."

             Pythagoras

Numerology Master Class - Practical

In this section of the Book of Number you will find step by step instructions for constructing a Numerical Chart.

It is VERY important you follow this through in the order in which it is presented. This is simply because every level of understanding builds to the next, and it is also the same pattern to follow when constructing a chart.

When you write up a chart for a person, there is a defined step by step process in how things are done.

Accordingly we construct the Practical Course to follow this order:

1. Fadic Numbers
2. Dominant and Composite Numbers
3. Noumenal Flow Chart
4. Cycles
5. The Matrix and Its Subsequent Aspects
6. Addendum Notes

By following this specific pattern you will gain a clear understanding of the facets of Pythagorean Numerology, and you will set up a template of sorts that allows to to move through to being able to construct a chart quickly and efficiently.

The Law of Number is: <u>One begets Two, which follows to the next</u>

In simple terms this means just going along, one step at a time, and allowing things to grow naturally. What will become of this present moment becomes the next by what you add to it. Every step of the journey in this book, when taken in the order it appears, is designed to help you grasp the step that follows it.

DISCOVER YOUR FATE

Your Fate Numbers are the basic additions that come from your Date of Birth and your Name. They are the Core Numbers from which almost everything else is based. Of themselves, they count for no great individual significance, but they are the cornerstones, or "keynotes" for the rest of the chart.

To arrive at your core numbers, you "add down" the basic numbers that occur in the date of birth, and in the name.

For example: Let's say you are born on 14 May 1987. This gives the number string to "Add Down" as: 1+4+5+1+9+8+7 = 35 We then "add down" the 35 (3+5) = 8. EIGHT is your BIRTH NUMBER

There are 12 Fadic Numbers, the numbers 1 to 12. These are the core numerals, of what is known as the Numbers of Creation. We also see them in the notes of music, and so many other areas.

Have you ever thought how often the Number 12 occurs in Western Civilization? We have 12 months of the year, our clock is divided into 12 hours, we had 12 Apostles, the 12 tribes of Israel, 12 Signs of the Zodiac, Shakespeare's 12th Night, 12 notes in music, etc.

However, in the context of Pythagorean Numerology, the DECIMAL SYSTEM is also a vital element. In Pythagorean Numerology we are running with a base 12 AND a base 10 numerical system. The solution has been to "split" the numbers One to Twelve into Lower and Higher. One to Nine are the "common" numbers, while Ten, Eleven and Twelve are "Higher Order" numbers.

For now, it is simply a matter of accepting these little quirks as we go through, and seeing how it all makes sense in the end. Classic "quirks" are how someone born on 24 Dec 1982 has TWO numbers to consider. (2+4+1+2+1+9+8+2 = 29 (2+9) = 11 yet 11 adds down to: (1+1) = 2. You have TWO Fate Numbers: Eleven and/or Two.

You will note I always write dates at day/month/year. This is the logical order and it is what we use throughout the book.

Adding Down

The First Step in all of this process is learning how to resolve a birth date or a name to a number that we can work with. This is very easy to grasp and is core to understanding Pythagorean Numerology.

We call the process "Adding Down" and in some books it is called Simple Arithmetic. Obviously, when dealing with a client, the first things we work with are their name, and their date of birth.

The Date of Birth is the simplest. If you are born on the Eighth of December 1967 this gives the numbers - 08 12 1967. Add these up and we get: 0+8+1+2+1+9+6+7 = 34

We then ADD DOWN the 34 as follows: 3 + 4 = 7

SEVEN is your FADIC NUMBER

A Name is resolved into number in accordance with the position of the letter in the alphabet. A = One, B = Two, and so on. We give the code for this here. It is known and the Magna Graecia.

A	B	C	D	E	F	G	H	I
J	K	L	M	N	O	P	Q	R
S	T	U	V	W	X	Y	Z	
1	2	3	4	5	6	7	8	9

Number values are given in accordance with the position of the number in the alphabet. For example: "J" is the TENTH letter of the alphabet: 1 + 0 = 1. "O" is the 15th letter: 1 + 5 = 6, and so on. (This also means each language has its own number value for letters)

As an example, the name "JOHN" becomes:

J O H N
1 + 6 + 8 + 5 = 20 which "Adds Down" to 2 + 0 = 2

ADDING INDIVIDUAL NUMBERS

NOTE that I add all numbers separately. The date 24/6/1943 could be added as 24 + 6 + 1943 which gives 1973, which adds to 20 into 2. It might seem like a small detail, but by adding the numbers INDIVIDUALLY the "real" sequence becomes: 29 into 11 into 2.

This is EXTREMELY IMPORTANT: Add each number individually to the next. I repeat: We always add up everything we find in a chart individually.

We are working with an evolved form of Vedic Math here. While any date adds down to the same last digit, there can be many changes in the Composite Number Values if we add things up in ways other than each number added individually to the next.

That said, write down the birth dates of people you know, and try practicing this simple first step. You will be doing this with every single chart you ever look at, so it pays to become proficient.

Example: 29 12 1967 = 2+9+1+2+1+9+6+7 = 37 into 10 into 1

Example: 12 6 1987 = 1+2+6+1+9+8+7 = 34 into 7

Everything we do in this course is done STEP BY STEP.

Every chart is a puzzle box. As we move through the additions and what becomes of them in a Step by Step manner, we discover the elements that make up the destiny of the person we are reading. Think of it as putting a jigsaw puzzle together, one piece at a time.

In keeping with the Pythagorean Tradition, we seek to resolve all things to simple elements, and to approach everything with the attitude of curiosity.

First: We find the Aspects and Patterns at work.

Second: We use common sense to work out what it all means.

Third: We explain this to the client in clear, unambiguous language.

How to Find the FADIC NUMBER

Just as you are born to a Sun Sign in Astrology, you are born to a Natal Number between 1 and 12. This is the basic FADIC (Fate) Number which we call the Birth Number.

This first step in any reading we do determines the "Key" number for an individual. It's a little like your Sun Sign in Astrology, if you will, and similar to establishing a "Key Note" in music.

This is a very simple thing to do: Just add up all the digits in any given date of birth, and do so individually.

EXAMPLE: Someone born on 13 April 1956 gives the sequence of: **1 + 3 + 4 + 1 + 9 + 5 + 6 = 29**.

29 is the COMPOSITE Number for the birth date of 13 / 04 / 1956.

We will deal with COMPOSITE NUMBERS in the next chapter, but for now, we want to REDUCE this down to what we call the Fadic Number. We use a process called "Simple Addition".

In this case **2 + 9 = 11** (Eleven)

Eleven is the Primary Birth Number, but here we already find our first complication. We need to go a step further, because 10, 11 and 12 are what we call "Higher Order Numbers" We add these down again to get a second Birth number. Obviously 1+1 = 2

The birth date of 13 / 04 / 1956 resolves to the series: 29 / 11 / 2

Similarly, the date 24 June 1943 becomes: 2+4+6+1+9+4+3 = 29. 29 (2+9) adds to 11 which adds down (1+1) to 2.

Which brings us to the first obvious question. *Do people with the same birth number share the same traits?* The simple answer is "not really". Just as there are a hundred songs written in the key of "G" that bear no great resemblance to each other, people who share the same birth number will generally have little that is specifically in common.

What WILL be shared are certain "keynote" characteristics such as with the 11 into 2 combination having a desire for study and/or an interest in politics, OR the curious opposite of these qualities, which is a sense of anarchy and the desire for beauty

Does this sound too complicated? Perhaps you are wondering how a desire for study and/or an interest in politics can be the opposite of a sense of anarchy and a desire for beautiful things? These don't sound very opposite, do they? In your study of Number you will learn many things that will surprise you. Let's take a moment, and look at just this characteristic aspect of the TWO.

A person strong in the energy of the TWO often has an interest in political matters. Yet basic physics teaches us that for every action there is a reaction. Someone strong in the Two energy may actively dislike politics, and they will generally either reject it (anarchy) or counter the political pressure around them with a deep appreciation of beauty. How are these opposites? Both politics and the appreciation of beauty require a *sense of comparison* in order to make a judgement of value. It's easy to see how anarchy is the opposite of politics, but taking the lateral step and grasping that appreciation of beauty as another "counter" is important.

One of the CORE VALUES of the Two relates to COMPARISON. The connecting thread between all these external aspects is comparison. Is this starting to make sense to you? You need TWO to compare. There is nothing to compare if there is just One, so when TWO appears, the first energy that comes of this is differentiation, or comparison. As you move through, and grasp the sense of what each number means, all this will start to make sense. It is rarely what you expect.

You don't have to work out what it all means. We have the Book of Interpretations for you to follow. Every Numerical Pattern or Aspect has a general description and is listed with the various (positive and negative, etc.) shades of meaning. But at the same time, you need to have a strong sense of what each number represents. This is a process that takes a minimum of six months.

For now we need to grasp the technical aspects and go through the physical process of resolving birth dates to number. The understanding of what it all means will come in due course.

Example: 23 Oct 1965 becomes: 2+3+1+0+1+9+6+5 = 27 which follows to 2+7 = 9. Therefore NINE is the Birth Number.

Just like a Sun Sign, a birth number gives a broad sweep definition of interests. When we look at a Nine Birth Number we often find someone who likes to run things, but who generally stays in the background. Nines tend to appreciate silence, and a sense of power, but of course, the flip side can be that they are inveterate chatterboxes who seem to have no clear focus or strength.

Example: 18 May 1988 gives: 1+8+5+1+9+8+8 = 40 = 4+0 = 4

A Four Person likes practicality, and for things around them to function. They dislike clutter and broken things, and enjoy the process of routine. They make excellent accountants, yet the flip side is the deep need to have no boundaries, and to travel the world with a backpack.

Example: 12 June 2010 gives: 1+2+6+2+0+1+0 = 12 = 1+2 = 3

A Three Person enjoys creative pursuits, conversations with strangers, and generally enjoys finding ways for things to connect in new and different ways. They also love to work with changing circumstances and different conditions, so they often do very well in self employment, their own business, etc. Yet the flip side is a tremendous fear of conflict, and to bury themselves in mundane positions, seeking to be invisible.

Summary: Each Birth date resolves to a number, and that number has a general indication of a direction. This is the first "keynote" to a chart and it sets the tone for all else that follows. It is like the Key a piece of music is written in, where all other elements in the chart are either harmonious, neutral, or dissonant to the Tonic.

General Knowledge Section

It is essential if we are to practice the Art of Numerology that we gain an insight into the meaning of EACH Number. Primarily, we have two basic "ranges" of number. These are the FADIC Numbers of One to Twelve, and the COMPOSITE Series which comprise the Numbers 10 to 53.

Numbers Represent Divine Truths

It is also important to understand that the Greeks looked at a Number not as a simple "One" or "Two" like we do in the West. Each number represented a doorway to an archetype or level of consciousness. A Number was really a NAME for an Aspect of Divinity. The number One did not mean just "one" as we currently understand it, but carried whole series of meanings ranging from Logos (Godhead) through to pigheadedness. All that was Singlular was touched by the energy of the One

Each Number has a RANGE of Meanings

Each Number has its own meaning. Furthermore this modifies like the flavour of a soup when different numbers (ingredients) are added to the mix. And every chart is a "soup"!

The meaning of any number in a person's life is defined by the numbers surrounding it. It is the <u>relationships between numbers</u> in any given chart that determine their meaning and consequence.

Given this, you as the reader need to have an understanding of the **range of meaning** each number represents. This Range of Meaning is far more than just Positive and Negative "attributes". We are talking about how you as the reader grasp Life's Basics.

Numbers represent basic life principles. Obviously, you need to have experience in life before you can really understand how any given number relates to it. It takes time. This book is here to assist you, but really, to understand life, you need to have lived.

You, as the reader, need to develop a sense of "interaction" with the numbers, so that the various combinations begin to 'talk' to you. As you build up a personal affinity with the meaning of each number, the chart before you becomes like a book you read. This will either come naturally to you, or you will need to learn it.

In this regard, learning Numerology is more like learning a new language. The more you practise speaking this language, the more you practise and play with it, the quicker you will learn.

Numbers as an "Alphabet"

English has an alphabet of 26 letters. Numerology has an alphabet of just 12 numbers. Just as letters combine into words, and words combine into sentences, so too does Number "string" together to form things that carry specific meaning.

It is important to grasp that Number is a LANGUAGE, with each individual number being a letter in that language.

In the first pages describing how we develop number from letters we see how to convert the alphabet to a numerical language. When you click into this "number language" you will look at a pattern of numbers in the same way you read a book. Things like a birth date and a name suddenly becomes an open doorway through which the shape of the person can be clearly seen.

As an example, a friend was trying to figure out Osama Bin Ladin's birth date. He contacted me, and we knew he was born in 1957. We narrowed it down to some likely dates that carried specifically a thing called a "Martyr's Cross" in the Vacant Position, combined with a Cruxifix in what is called the Stated Position. Only a few dates that year matched the energy and nature of the man. These were: 3/1/1957, 13/1/1957, 30/1/1957, 1/3/1957, 10/3/1957, 11/3/1958, and 3/11/1957. Turns out it was 10 March 1957.

When you understand the language of Number, you will hear the patterns and details of a chart "speak to you". But there is far more to it than just understanding patterns. A good deal of this study is learning how to explain things in a way that makes sense.

You can become the Keeper of the Flame

This is really a very simple study, yet it is very involved in the application. It requires a strong focus and attention to detail if you are to make sense of it all. It takes TIME to grasp the intricate nature of the Number relationships. You need to allow it to soak in.

Understanding every single piece of a jigsaw does not mean you will be able to solve it. We need to allow the greater vision to enter our heart and mind, and allow the illumination to come from within.

Your inner being has to light up, and by this light, you can share a spark that ignites another's heart to awaken. This book is a spark of light for you. It burns clear and strong, and all you need do is reach in and grasp it with both hands. Carpe Diem, dear reader.

All is Number

One of the famous sayings of the Pythagoreans was "All is Number". Number represents PURE ORDER. At their highest level, numbers are a representation of a higher force.

The "spiritual" number was known as Noumena by the ancient Greeks. "Noumena" represents an energy that occurs on a higher level of existence which echoes or mirrors here on Planet Earth as "Phenomena". In reverse, when you learn to follow the trail of numerical aspects in a chart, you will find that Numbers are "clues" left by the Gods that will lead you to a divine source of truth.

The Greeks define the Musical Scale by Number

The Greek teachings of ancient times related Number to all things. Yet the most direct and pertinent relationship the Pythagoreans made with Number was music and harmony.

The Greeks held that music was the highest of the Arts. But they also held that each note was in truth a symbol of NUMBER. That is, a sacred doorway through which the divine could flow. They named each note in the Twelve Tone Music Scale by Number: "A" was One, "B flat" was Two, "B" was Three, and so on. Music IS Number and the Greek Numbering of the notes is as follows:

Book of Number: Practical

A	Bb	B	C	Db	D	Db	E	F	Gb	G	Ab
1	2	3	4	5	6	7	8	9	10	11	12

This makes a good analogy for the way and manner in which WE need to see Number and number patterns: as a sort of Song. But in order to PLAY this song, we must develop the physical ability.

If you want to play music, a basic understanding of Music Theory is useful but not essential. But to play an instrument, you must have the physical ability to do so. That means putting in the hard yards and practicing. Same goes with reading charts. Do you have a burning WISH to do it, and the will to achieve this?

Numbers interact in exact accordance with Muscial Principles. As you can see in the above chart, the Number Four relates to the note "C", but this also relates to the "C" Scale. The "C" scale are the notes C, D, E, F, G, A, B. These notes can combine and create CHORDS: the major chords of "C", "F" and "G", as well as the minor chords of Em, Dm and Am. The chords of C, F, G, Em, Dm and Am sound totally harmonious when played with each other.

Unless you want to write a song, it's of absolutely no benefit for you to have this knowledge. Yet if you do, you can create whole symphonies using the Number Four as a base. Indeed, Beethoven, Mozart and all the great composers did exactly this.

From Simple Things, Great Things are Born.

Just as a note relates to a chord in a specific way, and one chord relates to another chord in music in a very specific way, in Numerology the relationships between Numbers are specific.

A combination of 1, 4 and 7 speak of a SPECIFIC energy. When combined with a different pattern, the harmonics generated are modified accordingly, yet also clearly defined. The core of this is simple. Grasp the PATTERN of Number in a chart, and you can then define exactly what the "song" that flows from this will be.

It will take time and application to understand this, but if you follow through one step at a time, it will unfold in a natural and relatively easy manner.

The Ancient Greeks believed Number contained the Power of the Gods. Many cultures have words for the Spiritual Force based on the attributes of Number. The Hindu Divinity, or Pantheon of Gods, is in itself a "Number System".

The Indian Sacred Music, the Rāgas, are all number systems, based on specific mathematical principles. Even the Hindu Chants are mathematical formulas. Did you know that "Om Mani Padre' Hum" is the tonal equation (or Sutra) for the Western Principle for "Pi"? All Ancient Vedic Math was, and still is, taught as SONGS.

I have witnessed a Vedic mathematician "Sing" a complex equation and write IN REVERSE the answer to this with an accuracy that measured to 67 numbers AFTER the decimal point. He not only beat an accountant using a calculator, he was more accurate.

When you see the patterns that evolve from Number sequences, you too will realize that there is a divinity in Number. The ancients associated this divinity with every aspect of their lives.

As you get more proficient at reading charts, you will find that you will surprise yourself as much as your clients. So often, a practitioner will go through someone's chart and say "This Aspect seems to indicate that this (specific thing) occurred in your life around age such and such." and the client will answer "How could you have possibly known that!!" It soon becomes obvious to even the most rank novice that there is SOMETHING at work here.

Numerology: We know it Works, but WHY?

Our study of Numerology is a little like a study of electricity. We may not know WHY it works, initially, but when we turn on the switch, the light appears. It is easier to just accept this.

At first we only need to know the mechanical process of how to work out a chart, and everything flows from there.

First, just grasp the mechanical process of HOW we generate a Pattern or Aspect in a chart, and then slowly it will make sense.

In time we may come to know WHY, but this may take some years. Even so, the first step in understanding the WHY is simply a contemplation on the meaning of the Twelve Sacred Numbers. So we come back to the FADIC NUMBERS as the CORE MESSAGE from which all Numerology grows. Learn the basics!

Meanings for Numbers.

I suggest a reading through of the core numbers, One to Twelve, in the Book of Interpretations. Try to start getting a feel for the internal and external meaning of each number in an overview

Your first exercise in regard to this is simply to practise working out the Birth Number of your friends and relatives. Soon you will start to assign some sort of meaning to their chart from the interpretation provided. Watering the garden, the seeds just grow.

The process again:

Add up their date of birth using Vedic Math, or what we call simple addition. Take someone you personally know, use their date of birth, add up all the numbers in it, and see what you can make of the interpretation for that number.

21 May 1972 is: $2 + 1 + 5 + 1 + 9 + 7 + 2 = 27$

Then ADD THIS DOWN: 27 become $2 + 7 =$ NINE.

Nine is the BIRTH NUMBER. We look up Nine in the following interpretations and we read some of the aspects of this Number, and what it means in a general sense. This is like reading someone's Sun Sign in astrology.

Note: Someone who "adds down" to 10, 11 and 12 has, in effect, TWO numbers that relate to them: $10 = (1 + 0) = 1$, $11 = (1 + 1) = 2$, $12 = (1 + 2) = 3$. Read both and decide which fits best.

Remember, our FIRST addition reveals a Composite Number, also listed in the Book of Interpretations, which we then ADD DOWN to form a Fadic or Fate Number.

Book of Number: Practical

Summary

Each Number denotes a specific frequency, or vibration that carries an energy. This energy exists on all planes of existence. These "vibrations" are also aligned with the colour spectrum, and the musical scale, but this will be taken up at a later time.

Initially we need to practise adding up the Numbers in our own and in our friends' birthdates. For now, just see how the description given with that number fits them, or not!

If it does not seem to suit, first make sure you have added ALL the numbers in their birth date, because many forget to add the "19" and write their birth date as: 23/5/54. It should read: 23/5/1954.

Also look at numbers that appear in any chart more than any other number, such as the two Fives in the above example, and read out the interpretation of this number to your friends. Ask them how this relates to them, explaining that they have more of this number in their birth date than any other.

In the next section in the Practical Study Book we will look at the area of COMPOSITE NUMBERS, which will help you understand the FIRST ADDITION of both the Name and Birth Numbers

After this we look at the Number Flow Charts that come from the interaction between Birth and Name energies. Following this we will look at the Pythagorean Matrix. It is at this time that the real depth of the study begins to shine through.

HOMEWORK:

Resolve the following Dates to the BIRTH Number:

12 Dec 1944

14 Jan 1739

31 Dec 1245

1 Jan 2001

The Sacred Principles of Simple Addition

- Life works by Addition (1+1=2) not multiplication (1x1=1). The joining of any two moments begets the next expressed reality.
- Any manifest creation, be it thought, emotion or physicality, draws towards itself an un-manifested likeness, as well as its opposite.
- Each choice the individual makes determines whether they join with the un-manifest likeness, or its opposite.

It may take you some time to grasp the above principles, but it is all wrapped up in the Law of Manifestation. This is essentially the principle "As above, so below" mixed with the understanding you can add to the present moment and alter both "above" and "below".

You may already get these ideas, or you may be trying to still grasp what is being said. Everything in these books will be absorbed and expressed through the individual in their own manner and in their own time. My only goal is to keep everything clear and accurate.

It is your own personal responsibility to acheive an understanding of all of this. Most have some idea inside the first few months. In my experience, if you simply focus and allow time for it all to sink in, you will eventually get the gist of what we talk about here.

It takes confidence and ability to become a practitioner. Yet even if you only work with friends, the experience of study and learning of this arcane wisdom will accrue significant benefits. It will also help you understand yourself, your family and your loved ones better.

When you are ready, move onto the next stage of study, which is:

DOMINANT and COMPOSITE NUMBERS

DOMINANT and COMPOSITE NUMBERS

DOMINANT NUMBERS

When any number is the most strongly represented Number in a Birth Date or Name, then that number becomes the DOMINANT or RULING Number. It's Number Weight is more than any other number present, so it has importance.

There are variations to this rule. Vacant Numbers can be put into the position of being a dominant, but we cannot cover ever single detail and subtlety in this book. However, as a guiding rule, the Dominant Number is the one that occurs most often in a chart.

In the date **19 Oct 1991** the number that appears most often is the ONE: 19101991 = FOUR One's and THREE Nine's. Therefore: ONE is the <u>Dominant Number</u>. Simple, yes?

Now, take a look and COMPARE the Dominant Number to the Birth Number, and we get a relationship to interpret... In this case, the birth number is: 1+9+1+0+1+9++9++1 = 31 into 4

Four is the Birth Number, and One is the Dominant Number of that date. Simple, really. No great difficulty with this part. The interesting part comes with understanding how each number interacts with other numbers. One and Four together create a specific energy.

These types of energies are described in "Doublets and Oppositions" in the Book of Interpretations. For someone with this birth date, it would be appropriate to look at the One - Four opposition.

But general knowledge also takes us to an understanding. The One is a very active number. A Dominant One likes to be busy doing something, and the Four is always looking for security and stability.

So if we are reading a chart for this person, the first thing we might ask is: "What do you like to do?" And following on: "Could you make any money out of this?"

Let's say that the person says they are happy making interesting furniture, and creating new designs. Well, we might then ask: "Have you tried to sell any of these any at the markets, or similar?"

Alternatively, you may find that in response to your first question, the person says they do nothing in particular. Then you might ask "Do you feel happier when you are busy doing something useful?"

Getting the idea? It is not just understanding what a number combination might mean, it is really more about extracting from the client what they are doing regarding the energy indicated.

Dominant Numbers give you a clue as to what sort of activity a person might prefer, and help you frame an understanding of where a person is at.

So ask the leading questions. If you have looked through the person's chart, you will already have some idea of the direction of things, but you need to qualify HOW this applies to the person in their day to day life. When you get a sense of where the client is internally, you are far better able to get a sense of what is needed.

In a summary of the One - Four / Dominant - Birth Number combination, I would suggest that the person is ideally:

1. Active with their hands (A keynote of the Dominant One) and
2. Using this activity to help their security and sense of adventure (Keynote of Four Birth Number)

Does it get simpler than this? We are looking for the OBVIOUS. Numerology can be very complicated in the details, but it is always about what is the most obvious, as that will be the most likely.

It is very easy to get carried away with complication, and we must continually bring ourselves back to simplicity and commonsense.

All "big" things are made from lots of "little" things. Every jigsaw comes from a thousand or so pieces until we fit it all together and the overall picture becomes self-evident

In modern terms, we call this practicing Occam's razor.

OCCAM's (Ockham's) RAZOR

The term "Occam's Razor" first appeared in 1852 in the works of Sir William Hamilton, 9th Baronet (1788–1856). In a nutshell it can be summarized as: "simpler explanations are, all things being equal, generally better than more complex ones"

Attributed to William of Ockham, the "razor" is a principle which states that the simplest explanation is often the most correct. He was the first economist, in one sense.

In *Summa Totius Logicae* he writes, *"It is futile to do with more things that which can be done with few"*. In other words, don't complicate things. Science uses this as a guiding principle in finding core truths in theories. You take the "razor" to different viewpoints, slicing away complication till you arrive at a point of similarity.

In truth, it should be called the Pythagorean Axiom, and the earliest extant practice of what we now call "Occam's Razor" occurred with Aristotle, who used Pythagorean logic to whittle large subjects down to manageable concepts.

We go into this in "Logical Fallacies". (Client Psychology book)

The point I am making here is that we need to KEEP IT SIMPLE. You see an aspect in a chart, so you QUALIFY how it applies to the person, then you use that information to work out how a particular aspect of the chart applies to the individual.

HOMEWORK:

Practice on your friends!! It is self-evident when one number has a strong representation in a chart. Just use their BIRTH NUMBER and see what other Number is DOMINANT in their date. As a note, there are sometimes two or more numbers that all have the greatest weight. Play with it, and see what people tell you as you go through the process.

The next stage of our study is: <u>Composite Number</u>

Composite Number

Composite Numbers are the series of numbers between 10 and 53. The Composite Number is derived from the primary "Add Down" from the Birth Date and the Client's Name.

1. 25 June 1956 = 2+5+6+1+9+5+6 = 34.
2. 34 is the COMPOSITE NUMBER.
3. We add this down further as 3+4 = 7

Summary: In the date 25 June 1956:
- 34 is the COMPOSITE Number
- Seven is the FADIC, or FATE Number

As you are practising on people, when you feel confident, start adding up the NAME numbers as well. I will put in the Magna Graecia (Great Code - next page) again to make it easy.

Our hypothetical client is John Peter Clark. We convert his name into Vowels and Consonants and add up the different additions to create a series of composites.

This system is always used in the Noumenal Flow Chart (next chapter). There is a specific reason WHY we separate Vowels from Consonants. Without putting too detailed an explanation into print, vowels are "unformed" tones, and consonants are "formed" tones. (They are made by the shaping of the mouth and tongue)

Now, as soon as I look at a number series such as we see on the following page, I know this will be a difficult set of energies for the person. In a normal reading, I am already asking questions about their life, marriage, what they do, what they hope to achieve. I want to build a bridge and create a sense of trust between us.

Listen closely to what people say. When the time comes to make suggestions, you want enough information about the person so that you can put things to them in a way they will understand.

Book of Number: Practical

John Peter Clark - Hypothetical Example

A	B	C	D	E	F	G	H	I
J	K	L	M	N	O	P	Q	R
S	T	U	V	W	X	Y	Z	
1	2	3	4	5	6	7	8	9

	6			5		5			1	6+5+5+1 = 17	17	8	8
J	O	H	N	P	E	T	E	R	C	L	A	R	K			
1		8	5	7		2		9	3	3		9	2	49	13	4
									1+8+5+7+2+9+3+3+9+2 = 49	66	12	3

So, we have the BIRTH numbers:

25 June 1956 = 2+5+6+1+9+5+6 = 34 into 7

And we have the NAME numbers:

Vowels: (17 into 8) plus Consonants: (49 into 13 into 4) equals

Name: (66 into 12 into 3)

We take this "field of numbers" concept a lot further when we look at the Noumenal Flow Chart, but essentially we have isolated a specific array of numbers to look at here. Now we can get a yardstick on what it may all mean.

I must stress again, these are preliminary steps that you take with every single individual. We generate a what amounts to the "energy field" that surrounds the person, and while every single aspect may not be significant, as a whole, every piece is part of the jigsaw.

If you want to read further in this specialized area, possibly the best book on the subject is Dan Millman's "Life You Were Meant to Live". It is recommended reading. For now let's look at John Clark.

Book of Number: Practical

Interpretation for John Clark (hypothetical)

34 into 7 (Birth)

Lone Wolf Type. Loves learning and reading. Often these people will be found to be keeping journals and even writing books. They are the "Dark Horses" who keep a lot close to their chest.

17 into 8 (Vowel)

In the VOWEL Area, which is expressed emotions, personality, etc. this pattern indicates a certain fragility. The person likes to build, but has little confidence it will be sustained.

49 into 13 into 4 (Consonant)

The Consonant Position indicates the Inner Self, and this series indicates the person tends towards being a little quirky and likely to be misunderstood. This combination of the 8 Vowel and 4 Consonant is really not a fortunate one. Added to the lonely sort of energy of the 7 we find the indication that this person's life will be difficult until they start to believe deeply in their right to be here.

66 into 12 into 3 (Name Combined)

Now, you will note that there is NO 66 as a Composite Number. The series goes to 53. Any number above 53 is either REVERSED or added down. (Ie: 92 becomes 29, 89 becomes 17)

66 adds to 12. (WHICH in turn adds to 3) Twelve indicates success after a long battle and great sacrifice. In essence, this is a person who must learn to become the hero. They must master their self-doubts and desire for seclusion, and rise above their fears to take charge of their external affairs.

If you look these aspects up in the Book of Interpretation, and read the complete summary, you will get the sense that this is an unfortunate series of Number. And it will be, but this changes when the person turns around and takes charge of their life.

So the message to John Clark is simply: *Turn around and take charge of your life.*

Additional Information:

Each BIRTHDAY represents a new cycle. This awakens the energy of the relative Composite Number as well. John Clark: born 25 June 1956. Birth Number is a 34 into 7. However, in the year 2013 the relevant date will be 25/06/2013 which adds to 19 into 10

As a reader, you compare the 19 to the Birth Number of 34 and see what picture forms in your mind. The 19 is an extremely fortunate number, and it indicates that a great deal of good fortune may be arriving to counter the otherwise unfortunate energy of the chart.

Composite Reversals and Adding Down

As noted, Composites range between 10 and 53. If a number is OVER 53, to find the composite meaning either REVERSE it or ADD IT DOWN to a lower number, as appropriate.

> Example: Reversed: 64 is interpreted as 46
> Example: Added Down: 127 is interpreted as 1+2+7 = 10

NAME Additions

As already detailed, we take the NAME, and resolve this down to Composite Numbers as well.

Using the Magna Graecia Chart we can easily ascribe number to letter. There is also a "short form" where we do not separate the vowels from the consonants.

So the example of the Name "JOHN" becomes:
J O H N
1 6 8 5 = 20 into 2

In the following section, the Noumenal Flow Chat, we will be looking closely at this addition process, but for the present, the normal practice is to add the VOWELS for a Name, and then add the CONSONANTS for a name. We then add these two numbers together to get the NAME VIBRATION, or Name Number.

Example: John Smith becomes the following:

```
  6          9         = 15 Personality
J O H N    S M I T H
1 8 5      1 4   2 8   = 29 Inner Nature
```

We then add the 15 to the 29 to get 44. 44 is the Composite Value for the Name.

We will look at all of this in far more detail shortly, but for now just get the idea of adding a Birth Date and a Name down to a series of Composite Numbers.

In short, each Letter has a Number value. We convert the Letter to a Number and add the Numbers together to form a Composite. Simple, really. You will get it in minutes with a little practice.

The Question of the "Y"

The Question of the "Y" is whether it is a Vowel of a Consonant. In simple terms, if the "Y" is used as a Vowel, add it as a Vowel, otherwise add it as a Consonant. (Foreign names often use a "Y" as a Vowel, as in names like "Kyster")

HOMEWORK:

Resolve these Dates and Names to their Composite Numbers.

John Jones
30 June 1956

Patricia Hamilton
14 May 1939

Gregory Dalton
12 Jan 1927

Next we move to the study of the Noumenal Flow Chart

NOUMENAL FLOW CHART

In this section of the course we start to get to what may seem a very complicated arrays of numbers, called the Noumenal Flow Chart. As always, move through a step at a time, and in short order you will see how it is all simple, logical steps.

The term "Noumenal" comes from an Ancient Greek term, and relates to the word "Number". The term effectively means the "Spiritual Value of Number" and is best expressed in the adage, "*From the Noumenon to the Phenomenon*". This is to say, from the unformed energy (Noumenon) to the formed energy (Phenomena)

This area of the Chart describes how Life Energy follows certain "Pathways" as it moves into the individual's conscious awareness. This area of the chart describes the pattern of energy as it flows from the Divine to the Manifest, or some might describe it as from the Subconscious to the Conscious.

We use the Hypothetical Name, and Date of Birth to construct a pattern (or grid) of numbers that looks like what you see below

	6			5		5			1			17	8	8
J	O	H	N	P	E	T	E	R	C	L	A	R	K	
1		8	5	7		2		9	3	3		9	2	
				Name Value								49	13	4
												66	12	3
2	5	0	6	1	9	5	6	(Birth Date)				34	7	
		DESTINY NUMBERS										100	19	1
		Number Flow			8	4	12	7	(19)			10	1	

We can see now that the Destiny Number, the addition of everything, is ONE. The FLOW is determined by the energy running through the various aspects highlighted, and it builds a picture.

Book of Number: Practical

It all looks complex, but it really is a step by step procedure.

- We take the Name, and separate the Vowels (Personality) from the Consonants (Inner Nature). We add down the value of the Vowels and the Consonants.
- We then add the Vowel and Consonant values to each other to get the Name Value. (Ancestral Energy)
- We add the Birth Date, and resolve this to Number
- We then add the Name Value to the Birth Number, which added down gives us the DESTINY Number.

This process continues until we add down all the various numbers in the Flow Chart to single numbers. Now we have a pattern of Number and can start developing the chart interpretation. The flow chart is like water running down a hill, except the water is energy running through a person's life, creating patterns of existence.

Let's look at a REAL person and see what develops. Peter gave his permission to use this, and when I first met him it was obvious he had a more challenging situation than most, as he was in a wheelchair. By asking qualifying questions I established he wasn't looking for miracle cures, but was looking for a direction he could take. It was evident to me he suffered a great deal of frustration and had a residual anger as a result of his situation.

	5		5				1		5				3			1			20	2	2
P	E	T	E	R	C	H	A	R	L	E	S	B	U	H	M	A	N	N			
7		2		9	3	8		9	3		1	2		8	4		5	5	66	12	3
Name Value																			86	14	5
BIRTH				1	1	0	1	1	9	5	5								23	5	5
DESTINY NUMBERS																109	19	10	1

Where do we start? Always look at the obvious. Can you see how many Fives and Ones there are in this chart?

Book of Number: Practical

We see a Dominant ONE in the Birth Date, and it adds to a FIVE. There is a Dominant FIVE in the Name, with a FIVE in Name Value and FIVE as the Birth Number. The Destiny Number is a ONE.

This immediately tells us that ACTION (One) and COMMUNICATION (Five) are very important to this person. The obvious is that the first is made far more difficult by him being in a wheelchair. This could easily explain the sense of anger I felt from my client.

This is a very odd chart. So much speaks of good fortune and yet the external appearance and manner of the Querent seemed to say the opposite. I qualified things further, asking direct questions. "The chart indicates financial windfall. Is this true?" (19 in the Destiny Area indicates money being gifted) It turns out that the accident that put him a wheelchair paid him a large amount of money.

The 12 Inner Nature tells of the need to sacrifice to attain, and the 14 in the Name Energy tells me simple communication will solve most things in life. Added to this, the 23 Birth Number is generally fortuitous, but only when clear communication is present.

Everything here spelled out LUCK in capital letters. Everything said "Communicate and all will flow for you" yet he was frustrated, angry and stuck in a wheelchair. Peter communicated this to me without words, but it was self-evident because I could feel the frustration. It was a puzzle, because it seemed self-evident he was having no luck, was not happy, and things were not working out for him.

It seemed to be one of the rare instances where someone was able to run counter to everything in their chart. But then it struck me. *What is it that Peter is communicating?* Everything I could read seemed to say he hated life, and he hated his situation.

Here was a person who, BECAUSE of their infliction, was gifted with huge resource. Yet he ignored that reality, he chose to ignore all that was good in his life and could only see the affliction.

I spent many years visiting Peter, but at each visit I saw darker and darker clouds gathering. He sat waiting for death on the beautiful farm he owned, in such a beautiful location, and in such misery .

Book of Number: Practical

He used the incredibly lucky Five energy in his chart, and communicated misery and loss. He blamed life rather than accept and work with it. Anger poisoned his good luck, and a lack of gratitude grew the bitter fruits of blame and recrimination.

There is nothing we can do when someone sets the sail of their inner ship to flounder on the reefs. There are no words, no actions you can take to steer another towards a better outcome, unless they inwardly want it. The Number Chart is a map. But it is the steps a person takes that determines where they go, not the map.

Every single person has two vases by their inner self, the Vase of Inspiration, and the Vase of Whispers. No matter what our chart may indicate, the choice we make every day, choosing inspirational thoughts, or dark whispers, this will eventually decide our fate.

Let's take another real life example. One of the most curious personalities in the world of politics was Richard Nixon. He "ruled the free world" as people say of the Presidency of the United States, yet suffered almost maniacal paranoia. He was a real life MacBeth.

9				1				9			1	3			9		6		38	11	2
R	I	C	H	A	R	D	M	I	L	H	A	U	S	N	I	X	O	N			
9		3	8		9	4	4		3	8			1	5		6		5	65	11	2
Name Value																			(49)	22	4
BIRTH				0	9	0	1	1	9	1	3									24	6
DESTINY NUMBERS												(127)		(73)			46	10	1

The first thing you see is that the Vowel and Consonants are BOTH adding down to Eleven. Many Numerologists call Eleven a "Master Number". In truth, it's just another number. What IS important is that the eleven repeats, making it more significant.

11 + 11 into 22 is a strikingly powerful aspect. It denotes a deep interest in, and a desire for, power and knowledge. A quick look at Nixon's flow chart gives a few interpretations.

38 into 11 Personality

This is a curious aspect of INERTIA. The weight of the past pushes you forward into the expectations of self, parents and your peers. It can give a sense of inability to choose your own path. However, the CURE for this inertia is to LISTEN.

Listening is a very important is we wish to resolve the lessons of this number. With the ability to listen comes the ability to hear clearly the inner voice. This leads to resolution of many problems.

11 into 2 Inner Nature

When the person affected by the nature of the Eleven finds a motivation, or a sense of purpose, they find they seem to materialize what they need to achieve it. However in the negative aspect it also indicates treachery and self-created difficulties.

24 into 6 Birth Number

Assistance and help will flow from above. Your connections will open doors, and your path may seem set. However, only if you stay true to yourself and those who have helped you, will things continue to go well.

46 into 10 into 1 Destiny

Excellent for those who commit themselves to projects. A person who dwells in the negative area of their consciousness will find a feeling of intense inner emptiness inside. Issues of addiction can result, and a deepening sense of isolation.

If so, you may be struck down in mid-career due to internal conditions, and unable to complete the tasks you have set for yourself.

Summary:

If Nixon were a client, I would advise him the greatest thing he could develop to balance out his chart was trust. Trust Life, go with the flow of things, and all will be well. He failed to listen to commonsense, and paranoia governed his actions. This led to Watergate, and to his downfall. Yet after all the negatives, he changed his ways, and came back into the kind regard of his peers.

Let's look at the process of creating Nixon's flow chart:

It is simply a matter of addition. If you can add, you can do this.

1. Resolve the VOWELS and CONSONANTS of the Name into their Number Values, and place them into the grid.
2. We add the Vowels to get the FIRST Addition of 38
3. We add the Consonants to get the First Addition of 65
4. We add these Values to get 103.
5. We add the Birth Date to get 24
6. We add the 103 NAME Value to the BIRTH 24, to get 127

The Next Level is to move to the SECOND series of Numbers.

7. We convert the 65 Consonant to 11. We add this 11 to the Vowel 38 to give us 49 (Name Value).
8. *49 Name and 24 Birth add to 73. It reverses to 37 Destiny.*
9. We add the VOWEL Value of 38 down to 11. Here we note that the 11 has already appeared TWICE.
10. 11 Vowel and 11 Consonant add to a 22 Name.
11. The 11 Vowel and Consonant add down to 2 + 2 = 4 (Name)
12. Birth Value adds to (2+4 = 6) 6. Added to the name is 4 + 6 = 10, which adds to a ONE DESTINY

What is highlighted is how the 73 in the Destiny Line of Richard Nixon is reversed to 37. If we look at **37** as a Composite in the DESTINY field, we see: *37 is a number of Bridge Building. It can create many connections people may have thought impossible.*

Who was the person who embraced China and created a bridge between Capitalism and Communism? Who ended the Vietnam War? Who was the President most recognized for his grasp on Foreign Affairs? Richard Milhaus Nixon.

This chart of Nixon was created many years ago, but as I read through it, I am once again struck by the remarkable way Number Patterns can map out a path that seems so clear, so robust.

Book of Number: Practical

Every individual on Earth has a flow chart. It all seems complicated but really, it is just following a process. The real secret is using the number flow as a clue, and listening to your inner voice. It will lead you to questions. So ask them! You will learn that ASKING QUESTIONS will guide you to a better understanding of the core issues at work. Ask questions and LISTEN CAREFULLY to the answers.

In this section I have given you a common theme. One individual is famous, the other unknown, yet both were equally vulnerable, and indeed fell victim to, their internal whispers.

Why do people fall victim to the inner negativity?

It is to do with what Scientology called "The Tone Scale". Every person exists at a different emotional level. Ranging from the high point of serenity of being, to the low of abject apathy, we slide up and down this Tone Scale in varying degrees every day.

The Pythagoreans spoke of two vases at the portal of each person's existence. One vase is full of Aspiration, the other is full of dark whispers. As a person goes out each day from their inner world of thought to the outer world of activity, they choose which vase they will draw from. (Refer: Book III - Client Psychology)

Social background, upbringing, education and parental influence create the elements that fill each vase, but we are the ones who choose what we take from the influences around us.

We can say with absolute certainty that the seed of an acorn will only produce an oak, but we don't know whether this potential oak will find fertile soil, be well watered, or find enough sun to thrive.

In many ways, the true task of a good reader is to provide information where the person can find the "good soil" within themselves. The job is to reveal the inner map so a person can more clearly choose the way they want to go.

Let the numerical facts speak for themselves. State them clearly, and let your clients decide the direction they wish to take things.

Different Format

You may note that other books on Numerology, if they use the number flow chart at all, often give a different meaning for each individual area. Let me take a little time to explain how we determine what each area signifies.

The Pythagoreans considered that the Individual had many levels. We all are Eternal Soul, a spark of divinity that moves from body to body, gathering knowledge and truth until it becomes perfected.

In each incarnation, Soul develops a personality. This personality transcends death, and continues learning on the inner planes. When the personality passes away, the Soul then incarnates again into another body, developing a new personality. This area of the personality is symbolized by the Vowels

Underneath this is a driving force, a series of karmic seeds that, in each incarnation, produces the inner nature of the person. This area is symbolized by the Consonants.

The vowel represents the unformed energy, the consonant represents formed energy. In physical practice the VOWEL is a natural sound formed in the larynx and the CONSONANTS shape these tones to create language. These are formed in the mouth.

Vowels are the core energy of language. Consonants shape this energy into an articulated form.

The combination of these two are reflected in and through the influences into which a Soul incarnates. A person's name is really a symbol of the stamp left by the parents on a person's life. Your NAME indicates the Ancestral Energy that governs a chart.

There are some who tag terms such as "Soul Urge" to aspects of this Flow Chart, and many other varieties, but the rose by any other name smells just as sweet. The natural difference between a vowel and a consonant remain unchanged. We interpret this as Persona, Inner Nature and the combination as Ancestral Burden or Energy.

SUMMARY

Vowels indicate: Personality

This demonstrates the expressed energy of the client

Consonants indicate: Inner Nature

This shows the internal process of the client

The Name indicates: Ancestral Energy

These are the forming energies around the client

The Birth Date indicates: Birth Number

This describes the immutable energies around the client

And everything added together indicates: Destiny

Which is the psychological destination of the client

Homework:

Practice working out the Noumenal Flow Chart of some friends and relatives. As a note, always ask permission to do so.

I suggest you take a copy of the grid included at the end of this chapter (over) and use this to assist you.

When you are ready, move onto the next stage of study: CYCLES

Please note: While your study get more complicated with variables from here on in, the step by step approach, taking each section as it comes, will keep things structured for you.

Book of Number: Practical

Magna Graecia (Great Code)

A	B	C	D	E	F	G	H	I
J	K	L	M	N	O	P	Q	R
S	T	U	V	W	X	Y	Z	
1	2	3	4	5	6	7	8	9

Sample Grid for Noumenal Flow Chart

- Personality
- Inner Nature
- **Ancestral Energy**
- **Birth Number**
- **Destiny**

CYCLES

In this session of the course we will be looking at Cycles.

Read through, get the basic idea of the principles, and keep the idea of Cycles in the back of your mind. These occur again and again as a core principle in understanding the nature of Number.

We interact with Cycles every day. You may not realize it, but every important event in your life is related to a series of cycles. These events were set into motion well before you consciously experienced them.

Cycles build on each other. Your next major event in life will have come about because of a previous Cycle, and its effect will start a new series of Cycles, and on it will go. The simple rule to remember is this: *Whatever anyone is presently experiencing is related (via the Law of Cycles) to some event that occurred in their past.*

You may have heard of Circadian Cycles, or rhythms? These are natural cycles set up in the body that affect us. Our most obvious cycle is the yearly one, defined by the circling of the Earth around the Sun. We have the Lunar Cycle, the Economic Cycle, etc. etc.

All things in life move in a circle, or cycle. The Seasonal Cycle affects our food supply. The Cycle of Work affects our monetary supply. The only question here is: can we understand, and thus alter, the way the cycles around us control our environment?

And the simple answer is: Yes.

Let's take a look at some of the most basic numerical cycles that affect us, and some of the techniques used in calculating them.

The first and most basic cycle we experience is called the Pivotal Year Cycle. This is when the numbers in the YEAR of our birth are added to make a composite number, which is added to the current year giving us a future date that is important to us in some way.

PIVOTAL YEAR CYCLE

If you were born on the 24 June 1956 the ONLY number we are interested is the YEAR of birth. How does it work? Very simple.

1956 adds to 21, 21 plus 1956 = 1977

The FIRST Pivotal Year for this date is 1977, and it is conditioned by the Composite Number the year adds to. 21 relates to "The Universe" in the Tarot, and it indicates that in this persons 21st year great achievement is possible.

Obviously, we are usually lining up Pivotal Years as a retrospective view, but we use the years highlighted to "chart a course" of what applies to the individual in these cycles.

We lay out the series of the following Pivotal Years in the same way we figure the first. 1977 adds to 24. 24 plus 1977 = 2001. 2001 is the SECOND PIVOTAL YEAR.

24 relates to great gains if the individual has been true to themselves, so obviously we would be asking the client what happened between 1977 and 2001.

2001 adds to 3. 2001 + 3 = 2004 is the Third Pivotal Year

2004 adds to 6. 2004 + 6 = 2010 is the Fourth Pivotal Year

2010 adds to 3. 2010 + 3 = 2013 is the Fifth Pivotal Year

2013 adds to 6. 2013 + 6 = 2019 is the Sixth Pivotal Year

2019 adds to 12. 2019 + 12 = 2031 is the Seventh Pivotal Year

And so on. The main point we are looking for is the CONNECTING THREAD between the earlier years, which allows us to predict what is likely in the upcoming Pivotal Years.

If, for instance, between 21 and 45 the individual feels like a failure, then the trend is set in the negative. We would be seeking to address the internal issues that caused an extremely fortuitous period to reverse. What happened to create the inner choices that led to this conclusion? The most likely answer is inside the meaning of the Composite, they were not true to themselves, but in what way?

Obviously, there is a long chain of closely connected years after this, and whatever was set up in the earlier cycles is destined to repeat in some way, unless the individual can see the core energy present, and redirect it.

This is a purely hypothetical situation. Right now we are here to grasp HOW to lay out the framework to see what Pivotal Years are being called up

We have a chart for all the Pivotal Years in the Book of Interpretations, but it is still important to be able to work them out. The Composite Number from the year addition rules the cycle so it is also important to be able to work this out manually.

Example:

1932 adds to 15, 1932 + 15 = 1947

1947 adds to 21, 1947 + 21 = 1968

1968 adds to 24, 1968 + 24 = 1992

1992 adds to 21, 1992 + 21 = 2013

Getting the Idea? We are lining up a series of years where important events will have occurred, and we ask the client what happened in or around those times.

Often they need a little reminding. "At 15, what were your interests? Did you do something significant, like move house?" Then see what happened at age 21 that connects. It can take time, but eventually you will find a connecting thread between all these dates.

Age Cycle

Another way of opening up what happened in the Pivotal Years is to look at the AGE they were at in the year in question. Let's say in the above example the person is stuck on what happened in 1968. He/she is aged (15 + 21) 36 in that year. Let's look at what cycles are self-evident in the 36th year.

To do this is so simple. You work out what MULTIPLES can be used to find that number. And there are a lot: 2 x 18, 6 x 6, 2 x 3 x 6, 2 x 2 x 9, 2 x 2 x 3 x 3. In 1968 all these cycles coincide with a pivotal year in the client. What happened at Age 2, 3, 6, 9 and 18 that relate to him turning 36?

The client most likely won't remember much about age 2 or 3, but you will be surprised what thread you will find with ages 6, 9 and 18. Then you go back to Age 15 and the first pivotal year, and find whatever connects to all of the above. There is always something.

Alternatively, if the pivotal year falls at age 24, the number of cycles to look at are: 2 x 12, 4 x 6, 3 x 8, 2 x 3 x 4, 2 x 2 x 2 x 3, etc. again, people don't recall age 2 or 3, but 6, 8 and 12 are generally fairly clear. As a note, we also find significant blockages at times. Some people simply cannot recall a certain age, possibly because it is connected to abuse of some sort. Don't push to hard. We are not psychiatrists, and you can set off strong reactions in clients.

The point here is that multiple cycles pointing to a single date means that a lot of energy is converging on that point. It adds to the weight of importance connected to the date.

The Holographic Universe

To get the gist of what I say here, we need to view the Universe as a Unified Field. Currently, the term used is "Holographic". The theory is postulated in a book called "The Holographic Universe" by Michael Talbot. This is recommended reading, and suggests that everything in the universe already exists in a substratum, which is "called up" by an alignment of energy.

It states that our experience in life is really more like a projected Holographic Image than any sort of concrete reality.

At any given point, all potential always exists. What brings some things to the fore, to our conscious awareness, is the CYCLE. A Cycle is a balanced point where two or more elements of existence co-exist. It is when two or more harmonious factors combine in a synchronous environment. It is at this point that an invisible door opens in our world, and the energy behind it flows through, and into our life experience.

At any point in your life when you have a clear, identifiable set of numbers that repeat, match or combine, then you have a doorway through which energy can flow.

Imagine, if you will, that we are standing in the middle of a vast field that has a large veil drawn all around it. At specific times, one area of the veil opens up to reveal another field we can walk into. If we do not, if we stay where we are, then at some other point in time and space, another area of the veil will open. And so on.

We are never forced to move into any reality that opens up, and in truth most often we choose not to, because we are imprisoned in specific ways of thinking.

I remember very clearly when, at age 17, a spiritual doorway opened. I was sitting beside a black lake, and saw tongues of flame burning upon it. I realized this was a dichotomy, something that should not exist side by side, but it was there regardless.

At this point, a jolly, happy monk came by with his small group of followers. He addressed me by name, and asked "Are you ready to leave yet?"

He pointed towards a door, and beyond the door was bright, clear sunlight and open fields. It was only then I saw that I had been living in a dark cave, and I felt a deep yearning within me to leave and travel in those open fields.

But I did not. I wanted to, I really wanted to, but I said, quietly, "I cannot, I have too much religion in me still."

I woke up in a type of shock. Sitting bolt upright, I knew this must have been a dream, but the real shock was that I had, at Age FOUR, already rejected the church I had been raised in. I made the clear decision at that time that this religion was not truth, and that I would have no part of it. And yet, in that moment I understood that despite my best efforts, guilt, self-loathing and fear had soaked in.

How so? The best cucumber placed into a jar of pickles will one day become a pickle. The question now was: How do I "un-pickle" myself? I spent the next 30 years answering that question, slowly unlocking and releasing the toxins I had been soaked in.

Even though I had NOT stepped through to the open freedom at the time, the inner cycles had aligned, and I now knew the direction I had to go in. Yes, I had too much religion in me, but now I knew it, whereas before I didn't. Now I could work to solve the problem, and there were many layers to work through!

Cycles represent nexus points in time and space. They are zones of increased power where we are faced with a choice. Do we move forward, do we stayed tied to where we are, or do we retreat?

This is how Cycles work in our life: All potential is around us, but the CYCLE represents the opening of the door, or the parting of the veil, to a new potential. If we are listening to inner inspiration, we choose a positive frequency of experience. If we choose our inner whispers or fears, we imbue a negative frequency into our world experience. (Refer: "Vases at the Portal" Client Psychology)

Cycles themselves are things of a subtle, yet powerful, influence. They are like the air we breath, in that we are so used to their effect, we hardly notice them at work anymore.

This is an exercise in helping you be more aware of cycles: Write down major events that happened in your life. Record the exact date, if you can, and then move the clock forward three years, seven years and twelve years. See how events that occur in these time frames connect back to the original event.

Almost every time you will see how a correlation occurs that links the various apparently random events into a single "Cycle Line".

I cannot emphasize enough the importance of understanding how CYCLES affect us.

Numerology is all about Cycles that harmonize with, cancel out, or oppose each other. When you fully grasp this, all the aspects of this course will become extraordinarily clear.

A very simple technique to working out what cycles may be at work in your life right now is simply to see what the multiples of your present age might be.

Age 40 is 4 x 10, 2 x 20, 4 x 5 x 2, 2 x 2 x 5 x 2, and 8 x 5

At its core, ignoring the 10 and 20 as they compress to One and Two, there is a 2, 4, 5 and 8 at the base of the number 40. This connects forward to Age 42, 44, 45 and 48. At Age 40, 2, 4, 5 and 8 will reoccur again and again in some way. This is universal. If you are looking backwards from age 50, what came from the time at Age 40 that relates to these years in your life?

Take ANY DATE where something important occurred, and resolve what was your age at that time into whatever cycles are represented. And just like Vacant Numbers in a chart, there is great importance where there are NO CYCLES present. In Math, these are called PRIME NUMBERS, numbers only divisible by One.

If an important date is at an age that represents a Prime Number it indicates a start point of significance. Pay particular attention to what came about in your life during that specific time and place.

Major Life Cycles

To understand all the cycles at work in someone's life we would need to take an entire book on it's own. For the present let us look at the basic Cycles at work in everyone's life.

For the most part, each cycle is measured by constants, such as the rotation of the Earth around the Sun. Inside this cycle is a cycle of FOUR, the seasons, the cycle of TWELVE, the months, and the Cycle of FIFTY TWO, the weeks.

The main reason for 52 being the last Number in Composite Series is simple. There are 52 weeks in the year! It is simply that 364 divided by 7 equals 52. The Leap Year and the extra day are the consideration for the 53 that we use.

Outside the Yearly Cycle we have a series of numbers that are important. If you look at any mathematical sequence, but specifically the Fibonacci Sequence, and plot these against the life of an individual you will find correlations.

Life follows mathematical patterns. The shape of a flower, the shape of a coast line all follow mathematical ratios. The shape of the Nautilus shell is famous for how mathematical perfections are described within it. As Pythagoras said: All is Number.

There are no random events that do not fall within the broad embrace of mathematics, and when you understand the patterns within something, you can accurately predict the outcome.

I can confidently predict that the acorn will become an oak because I know that the pattern of life within the acorn can only have one outcome. I cannot predict if the acorn will be well watered, or if it will germinate, or if it will find good soil, but I do know that if these are provided, there is every chance it will grow to become an Oak.

It is the same with numerical facts. I can say with absolute certainty that someone with a Vacant 4-6-8 Trine in their Birth Chart will always have the desire to be self-employed. It doesn't mean they will be, or will be successful if they are, but this desire will be there.

So it goes with cycles as well. We have all heard the term "Seven Year Itch". And guess what, every seven years our body undergoes a complete recycling of cells and is in effect, born again. So often a marriage will break apart in the Seventh Year, and this is where the axiom comes from. But no one knew when they coined the phrase that there were direct, physiological realities behind this change.

Let's take a brief look at the major cycles at work and give a general description of the energy at work behind the scenes.

If you do not change direction, you may end up where you are heading.

Lao Tzu

The ONE Year Cycle

The ONE Cycle is about Focus and Commitment

This is of course the normal yearly cycle, but in Numerical terms, it relates to the energy of the birth date and is a core cycle at work in our lives. This cycle is always all about what you DO! Remember the New Year promises we all make about how we will change? Well, that facts are that precious few people actually succeed in changing anything, but only because they are not that focused or genuinely committed to change.

The TWO Year Cycle

Two Year Cycle relate to Relationships.

These are all about what is "becoming". Every time our age is in Even Numbers, we ideally will look at how we are relating to people, how we connect, and what we are creating as a result. We hear about the "Two Year Honeymoon" period of a marriage? This is absolutely true. At some point as the Two Year Cycle kicks in, people start looking at what they agreed to, who they married, and where it is going. Many marriages break up at this point because one or both partners realize it isn't going anywhere.

The THREE Year Cycle

Three Year Cycle relate to Family

This is known as the Metal Cycle and is an extremely important cycle on a personal and family level. Every three years a person starts to shift in frequency. You have heard of Silver and Golden anniversaries, etc.? These shifts and changes are moving around energies associates with specific metals.

Now, simply due to space restrictions I have had to condense the original course down and cannot give all the small details about such things as the Metal Cycle as I might wish. For those who wish to undertake higher study I will make these things available.

The main thing about the Three Year cycle is simply that it is a time to reassess and reassure family members. It is very important that a child's third, sixth, ninth and twelfth birthday has as many extended family members as possible around them on that date, as one example.

Your metabolism has a shift every three years, so it is also important to consider diet and even where you are living every three years. On every birthday that is a multiple of three, look at family, job and everything you are doing, and refocus.

The FOUR Cycle

This relates to Internal Moods and Outward Adventure.

The Four cycle is about moods, setting down roots, finding the square peg for the square hole and generally fitting in. Internally, the Four Cycle also relates to the natural shifts every three months, which occur according to the seasons. Externally, every Fourth year is a good time to take an extended vacation to somewhere new. On every birthday divisible by FOUR it is a good idea to set plans to have some sort of adventure.

The FIVE Cycle

This Cycle relates to Communication

So often someone starts an extended affair in the Five Year Cycle. It is all about communication, and by the fifth year of a marriage, this is often sadly missing. The person simply looks elsewhere to find a natural spontaneous connection with another. The Fifth Month of May was about Beltane, and during that time the Celtic people could sleep with whoever they wished to.

Fact is, human jealousies were as ripe then as they are today and it could be the source of furious divisions and arguments, but when you think about it, the argument is simply abrasive communication.

If you want to keep the marriage, pay loving attention to your partner. If you do not, the Five Cycle will often break you apart.

The Six Year Cycle

This energy is all about building

In the Sixth year of marriage, people often shift house. They have accumulated assets, and now want to move on to something bigger and grander. The Six cycle also often indicates the start of families created during a successful Five cycle, and so more rooms are needed.

This is the most fortuitous cycle to start a business in, or to expand on what you already have.

The SEVEN Year Cycle

This indicates breathing in, contemplation and wisdom.

The Seven Year Cycle either breaks or makes a marriage. People go past the petty things, and start to get to core values. Likewise, internally the Seven represents the ripening of the fruit before harvest. The inner life of potential is starting to wake up and take its place in the sun.

This cycle is all about claiming your place in the sun.

The EIGHT Year Cycle

The Cycle of Harvest

If you have been productive, energetic and working to build for the last seven year, this is an amazingly fortuitous period for you. If you have been lazy, the chickens come home to roost. As an example: The G.F.C. actually occurred in 2006. It was not felt fully until 2007 but the process of collapse started in an Eight year. The destruction of the financial system started with the removal of guidelines on the issuing of CDF and OTC derivatives some 7 years earlier.

Warren Buffet referred to this in his famous 2002 speech in which he warned against "weapons of financial mass destruction." These useless, non-production creations with nil inherent value were the cause of the world waking up to the shock of financial ruin.

Yet the Chinese, being industrious, hard working, and focused on creating things of substance were not touched by the global panic and indeed this period is a point where they surged forward.

On a personal level, you need to have prepared for the Eight year in a similar fashion. If you have, all will be well.

The NINE Year Cycle

New growth and the ending of the old come together.

The GFC in 2007 was clearly the end of the old, and the start of the new in our culture. Those who were willing to extinguish the past released themselves to begin anew, and this is what the Nine Cycles is all about. Letting go, and embracing the winds of change.

Nine is about governing your thoughts and emotions with silence, and likewise, this cycle is one of collecting your inner power and learning to re-apply what you have learned in the past to new goals for the future. Every Nine years, look to your long range plans and always be prepared to just start again if the direction isn't true.

(Note: The author predicted the Global Financial Crisis in 1993, base on the principle of Cycles)

We include a comprehensive listing of the major cycles at work in the Book of Interpretations. In the next chapter we are working on what amounts to "disguised cycles". Inside the pattern of numbers in what we call the "Matrix" is an application of Vedic Math that compresses the numerical information into cycles. This is a core, essential and extensive study that is the heart of Numerology.

Next: Understanding the Matrix

Book of Number: Practical

MATRIX STUDIES

The Nine Gods of Egypt

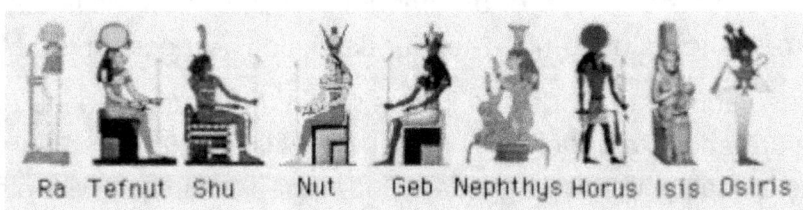

Ra Tefnut Shu Nut Geb Nephthys Horus Isis Osiris

Above is a pictorial frieze of the basic Nine Gods of the Egyptians. It is important to understand that these primary Gods were worshipped as POWER FLOWS in Ancient Egyptian thought.

In other words, by dedicating yourself to a specific God, you could bring that power into your life. The idea was to select the type that fitted your nature, and then go with it.

The early priesthood training is described very well in a 1930's book by Joan Grant called "The Winged Pharaoh". Essentially, the training involved out-of-the-body projection and, through this practice, becoming aware of the Inner Planes of existence.

The Egyptians had a Decimal System at work in their prehistory, even though their priests and guilds also used the Base 12 System in the sacred calculations.

The Nine Gods represent the principle of Number, as seen here. This is one of the patterns that Solomon used in one of his famed rings, and can be drawn as three triangles. Note: The seven pointed star ring of Solomon refers to the Diatonic Scale in Music.

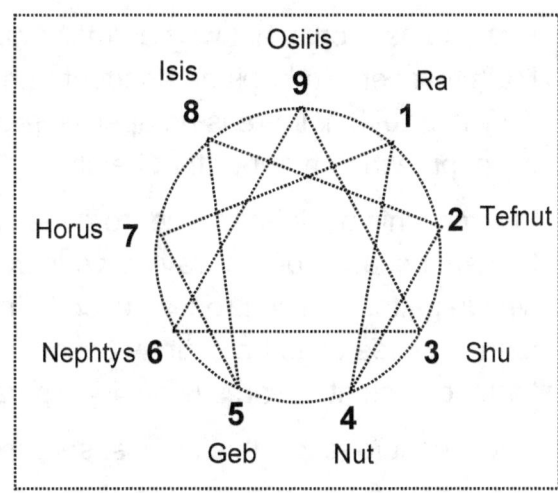

Book of Number: Practical

There is a clear thread between the numbers in the Ennead and the patterns we will soon discover in the Matrix. Go along any number in the graphic of King Solomon's seal, and move around the circle in sets of 2, 3, 4 or 5 numbers at a time. You will find the same patterns of number appear as distinct Aspects in the Matrix

These equate to Lines and Trines within the Matrix, the study which we are about to undertake. How it works is simple. Each number has a quality, like the Egyptian God. When combined with other numbers, they unite with the energy of each number to form a "new being", or more to the point, a new state of being.

There are 84 Trine and Line Aspects in the Matrix. These relate to the 84 Lacs (or ages) of existence in the Hindu teaching. How we discover all this in a Date of Birth, etc. we will come to shortly.

Essentially, the Matrix as we know it today is derived from the "Magic Square" principle. This is a perfect mathematical model where all the ancient ratio and math equations could be derived.

Vedic Math is the most extant form of ancient math still practiced. It can still be studied and there are some truly excellent books on the subject now in print. It is the closest thing to Pythagorean Math I can find. Vedic Math makes mathematics a SONG, and even a brief study will make you shake your head and wonder WHY school math was made so hard for us in the West.

Pythagoras, from what we can make out, must have had a Vedic Math teacher. Perhaps he encountered this during his time in captivity in Babylon, there is no specific record, but it very clear from his approach to number that he studied Vedic Math.

We know his work is derived from the same source as the Vedic System because of the way he adds down complex numbers to simple patterns. The process used in the Pythagorean form of Numerology seems to be entirely based on the form of Lateral Logic that the ancient Indian system incorporates.

If you want to follow this up, just search "Vedic Math" in Google.

The MATRIX: History

The Matrix represents a Crossover Point in the Ancient World, where the basis of Mathematics went from complex formulas reserved for neophytes and apprentices to a more understandable format for the common man

This change cannot be underestimated as to its impact. What this meant was that the complex, involved equations that normally took a student 12 years to master could now be taught in under a year.

THIS CHANGE IS WHAT ALLOWED PYTHAGORAS TO MOVE KNOWLEDGE OUT FROM THE GUILDS AND INTO THE HANDS OF THE COMMON PEOPLE.

Since time immemorial, protected Guilds and the priest-craft had frozen knowledge into segregated parts of the community. If you wanted to build a house, you needed a mason, a "rope stretcher" (geographer), a priest and a few other "specialists" to come in and qualify every aspect of what you were doing. This was expensive.

Pythagoras introduced a mathematical model that allowed the one builder to do it ALL. He streamlined knowledge and made it more accessible. This changed the way the world worked. Pythagoras took ancient knowledge out of convoluted, arcane thought, and placed it into simple, easy to grasp principles that anyone could understand and apply.

Moreover, he also introduced the original scientific method of "test and proof". Yet for all the remarkable things he achieved, the thing he never invented is the one mathematical model everyone remembers him for: The Pythagorean Theorem.

Do you remember this from School? The 3 - 4 - 5 theorem is really a mathematical PROOF that Pythagoras introduced that allowed the common man to understand how basic geometry worked. The knowledge had long existed with the Egyptian "rope stretchers" and in India but Pythagoras took information from the grasp of the Guilds and Priests, and put it into the hands of ordinary folk.

Book of Number: Practical

The Core of the Matrix evolves from what we know as "Magic Squares". These are mathematical perfection where all numbers in a set of nine are in perfect balance to each other.

Magic Squares can be extrapolated to form ratio equations, logarithms, and many core mathematical equations. They are the heart and soul of all early math, and have been found in ancient manuscripts in China, India and the West.

Pythagoras used this form as the base for a simple pattern that contains all the elements possible within the Decimal System. While he is most recognized for the tetraktys, another "proof" of the Decimal System, for our numerical divination we use the simple "noughts and crosses" pattern that is called "The Matrix".

The Number Matrix

The Pattern is like the "Noughts and Crosses" game

3	6	9
2	5	8
1	4	7

Number Positions in the Matrix

Each of the vacant "squares" is given a number value and when that number is represented in a chart, it gets a "tick" every time it appears in the appropriate box.

The Original "Magic Square" where this derives from was comprised of numbers arranged so that every line added to 15, but this was altered for the sake of simplicity.

The History of the Matrix/Magic Square is long and involved. If you care to go into it more thoroughly (and note that this is not necessary for reading a Chart) check out the online resource at the bookofnumber.com.au website. We have a short essay on the subject, but for now, a simple overview is all that is needed.

Once you grasp how Number forms pattern, and how this has significance to the individual, you will start to see the amazing value of the Matrix. Number patterns thrown up by random events are captured by this simple tool.

Book of Number: Practical

Historical Snippet:

Most of us know about the Golden Age of Greece. It is the root from where current principles of democracy, free enterprise, philosophy, education for all, and religious freedom spring from.

But the Greeks didn't receive their knowledge like Moses being given the Ten Commandments. No stone tablets were handed to them from the Gods. Like the present day, students received knowledge and information from written records, and teachers. Most notable of these are the Papyrus scripts available only to the chosen few who were allowed to study in the Egyptian Temples.

When Egypt was conquered, many of these scripts (along with Pythagoras who was studying there at the time) were taken to Babylon, and from there the information spread out to the world. When Pythagoras was permitted to travel back to Greece, he brought with him a font of knowledge in the form of scientific and philosophical wisdom. Yet more importantly, he also brought the concept that claims in science and philosophy should be tested and proven. He established the first principles of the scientific model.

Despite being named after him, the famous "Pythagorean Theorem" was not invented by the man. He garnered this from far older sources, and like so much other knowledge, he condensed an ancient truth into the easy to grasp principle we know today.

The diagonal chord of the rectangle makes both the squares that the horizontal and vertical sides make separately.
— ***Sulba Sutra*** *(8th century B.C.)*

The square of the hypotenuse of a right angle triangle is equal to the sum of the squares of the other two sides.
— ***Pythagorean Theorem*** *(6th century B.C.)*

Book of Number: Practical

The Matrix: Basic Introduction

An essential part of Pythagorean Numerology is what we call the Matrix. It is not related to the movie, "The Matrix" (other than the movie is a good expression of many Pythagorean principles. As an example: All life is Number)

The Matrix we are talking about is a sort of "Noughts and Crosses" (often called Tic Tac Toe) Pattern that holds deep Mathematical and Spiritual significance. The Pythagoreans came to it from a study of Vedic Math, and more specifically, that which we call the "Magic Square" in Western Mathematics.

An area of ancient wisdom is, suitably, one of King Solomon's Rings. These rings were really patterns of truth, and the one below is really a description of energy flows in the Magic Square principle. From this particular pattern we can derive all our Numbers and our Alphabet.

KING SOLOMON'S RING

The Pattern on one of King Solomon's rings appears absurdly simple, but it carries deep significance.

Solomon Ring

This Pattern is a template of the Energy Lines in the Matrix. From this we can also derive every letter of the Alphabet and every Number is represented in there when we look for it. (See Below)

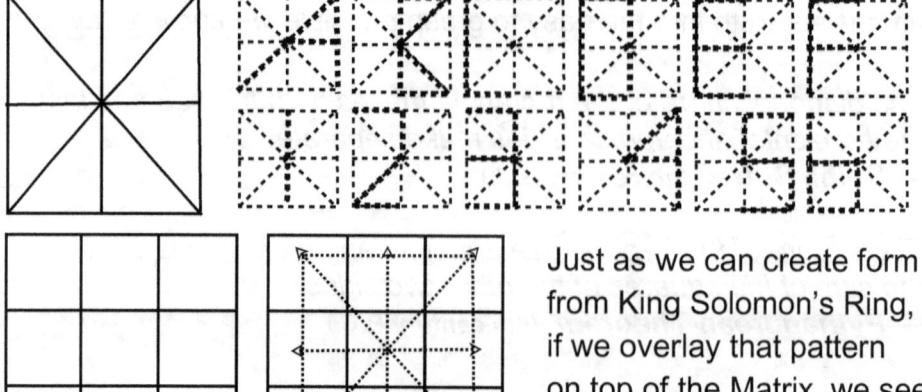

Just as we can create form from King Solomon's Ring, if we overlay that pattern on top of the Matrix, we see the basic "flows" inside it.

Book of Number: Practical

This Pattern describes the ENERGY FLOWS in the Matrix. As mentioned, the Matrix itself is like a "tic tac toe" pattern, with nine boxes. Each "box" is assigned a number value as described below.

This nine box graph is a visual way that allows us to quickly grasp where the number patterns occur in any individual chart. It is the heart and soul of Pythagorean Number Divination.

Working out the Matrix: Overview

If we think about it, a calendar date is simply a number pattern that expresses and contains a specific series of CYCLES. Every date has a series of cycles connected with it, and the Matrix is a fast way to see clearly what cycles are at work in this date.

We use the Matrix for both Dates of Birth and Names. For the name, we have already worked out Noumenal Flow Chart, and now we transfer the number values from this to the Matrix. We tick each number as a "weight" in the appropriate position in the Matrix.

This process is deceptively simple, but make no mistake! At the heart of all of this is sophisticated Vedic Math. Let's not get cluttered with details, but move on to the practical application.

If someone is born on the 15 May 1976 they have 2 x One, 2 x Five, 1 x Six, 1 x Seven and 1 x Nine (15 / 5 / 1976) in the date of their birth. We take the Number Grid described above, which gives us the position where to place the mark that now indicates where the WEIGHT of the Number lies, thus we find:

3	6	9
2	5	8
1	4	7

Number Position

Birth Date

15 5 1976

	6	9
	55	
11		7

Birth Numbers

	/	/
	//	
//		/

As Strokes

Book of Number: Practical

You can keep the Matrix Pattern using the actual numbers if you wish, but later on when we start combining Matrix Patterns of Names and Birth Dates, it can start getting very cumbersome. It is much easier to simply use Strokes

That is it! We now have the Matrix Pattern for the date: 15 May 1976. It is the SAME Pattern for the day 15 May 1967, and the SAME Pattern for the day 16 May 1957. Even the 17 June 1955 has the same pattern!

Why? All these dates carry the SAME WEIGHT of NUMBER in them. This is the ONLY thing we are interested in. The WEIGHT of number and where it is represented is what is important here.

This is the part many have difficulty with. The Numbers themselves are unimportant, only the weight (or repetition of number) matters. And it gets even trickier, because the Numbers that are NOT there are significant as well. These "Vacant Numbers" form patterns in the Matrix that have portent and meaning all on their own.

Number Weight in the Matrix (Noumenal Weight)

Let's go over this again, because it is of core significance to all that follows. Each number is given a "weight" according to how many times it is represented in a date or a name.

Yet obviously Vacant Numbers also share a zero "weight". On the date 15 May 1976 the numbers 2, 3 , 4 and 8 are NOT present, therefore they share a common (vacant) "weight" of zero.

The series of numbers that ARE represented (which we called "stated" Numbers) all carry a weight as well. The position of the "One" in the matrix (derived from the 15 May 1976) has a "weight" of TWO. There are TWO x One's in that date, so the "one position" gets TWO STOKES.

There are TWO x One's, TWO x Fives's, and ONE x Six, Seven and Nine. There are NO Two, Three, Four or Eight's present. So the One and Five have equal weight, and the six, seven and nine also share equal weight, as do the vacant Numbers.

Book of Number: Practical

When ANY Number shares an "Equal Weight" with any other number, there is a connection that has relevance to the chart.

In the 15/05/1986 Matrix:

1. The numbers 6, 7 and 9 share a weight of "one", thus have a relationship. (Called a "Trine" in this instance)
2. The Numbers 1 and 5 share a weight of "Two"
3. The Numbers 2, 3, 4 and 8 all share a weight of zero.

All the EQUALLY WEIGHTED Numbers (Vacant or Stated) form specific patterns that can be interpreted, however, the guiding rule is that unless there are THREE EQUAL WEIGHTS, the connection is weak. There are exceptions to every rule, even so, and we will look at these later in the course.

In the 15/05/1986 Matrix below we have the following Weights:

	/	/
	//	
//		/

1 / 5 (Not three equal weights: Weak)

6 / 7 / 9 (Called a Trine: Strong)

2 / 3 / 4 / 8 (Contains 4 Trines: Strong)

All these numbers have a relationship with each number that shares the SAME WEIGHT as it holds in the Matrix. Numbers that are NOT there can ALSO carry great significance! The Matrix shows the weights of number in any given date of birth or name.

Vacant Positions

As we have mentioned, the numbers that are NOT represented can be as important as those that are. In the duration of this course we will show you how to understand and resolve ALL Vacant and Stated Numbers into their relevant Patterns and Aspects.

Vacant Positions tends to reflect the subconscious, or hidden, aspects that drive a person. They are very powerful, because they affect the individual from below the surface of conscious thought. It is like the Taoist saying: *Why does the King of the Ocean rule? Because he rules from below.*

Even though this information has been available, and proven, for the last 22 years in the public domain, we still find very few people focusing clearly on the importance of the Vacant Position. Vacant aspects are of the very greatest importance!

The strongest weight is also important. In the chart maps below I have "looped" the "line" which has the strongest weight of number represented on it. This is called a "Line of Force" and is another of the recognised aspects of reading a Matrix Chart.

Now, we have noted that there are FOUR Vacant Numbers in the 15/05/1976 Matrix. These FOUR numbers have four possible combinations of THREE EQUAL WEIGHTS. This is what we call a TRINE and this group of aspects (84 in all) form the heart and soul of Matrix Interpretation.

Numbers 2, 3, 4 and 8 can be shaped into the following combinations of three. 2/3/4, 2/3/8, 2/4/8 and 3/4/8. I show these as a graphic to make certain this aspect is perfectly clear. It is the core of our study to grasp the way we evolve Trines from the Matrix.

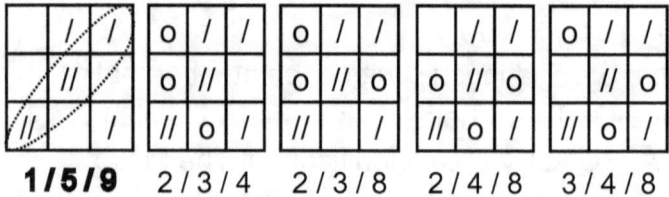

Each "o" represents a Vacant Number and it's position

1/5/9   2/3/4   2/3/8   2/4/8   3/4/8

The Various Lines, Trines and Patterns in the Matrix:

So, we can now go to the Book of Interpretations and see what each of the aspects for the date 15/5/1976 will be. Now that we have an array of Trines, what we have is INFORMATION.

The list of aspects in this date are: 1/5/9 Line, 6/7/9 (Stated) Trine, plus 2/3/4, 2/3/8, 2/4/8, 3/4/8 (Vacant) Trines.

Book of Number: Practical

The "1/5" is called an "Opposition" but without other matching oppositions, it is extremely weak. In this case, its energy is "eaten up" by the stronger 1/5/9 Line of Force.

An extremely brief summary of 15/5/1976 is as follows:

1/5/9 Line of Force

Indicates a will to succeed and the driving force to overcome all obstacles, but not the actual motivation to do so.

6/7/9 Trine

Six-Seven combination comes into conjunction with the Nine, and gives a pervasive aura that can penetrate the darkness of man's superstition.

2/3/4 Vacant Trine

A Soul with this aspect in their chart has the ability to make money from their creative impulses, and yet there is often a conflict here: Where the person just wants to "BE" and not involve themselves with the financial aspect at all.

2/3/8 Vacant Trine

Financial ability and courage are needed. The individual needs to rise above their fears, and really go for it. If they can, great success will come.

2/4/8 Vacant Trine

Principles must be adhered to if life is to work out well for this aspect. There is a cat-like survival nature at work here, but there is also humour and friendship. It is important that these people find a work environment to suit their temperament.

3/4/8 Vacant Trine

There must be developed a "carry on regardless" attitude for success here, which, if done, will unleash the power of creativity in every aspect of the person's life. This can solve almost every problem, some before they even arise.

Can you see how the Matrix has created an "instant map"? It starts to define specific characteristics and details areas the individual needs to focus on, if they are to make a success of their life.

Information on the 8 x Lines of Force is relatively common, but the interpretations on the 76 Trines have not been published anywhere (other than by myself) since the 1820's.

Precious few numerical systems deal with any accuracy in this area, and fewer still go into anything like the detail and length we go to here, with all the aspects, as taught by Pythagoras.

The area on Patterns that we take up later had not been published in over 1400 years. This is another extraordinarily accurate and powerful tool for Divination and Analysis.

Lines in the Matrix have been well covered in other books, but even here the information was less than complete and we have attempted to bridge this gap as best we can.

This brief overview of Matrix Chart Analysis will prepare you for the more complex aspects to follow.

Overlay Patterns.

The concept of OVERLAY Matrix Patterns is so terribly obvious. We overlay the various patterns that emerge from a chart, so we can see how they match up with the parent's Date of Birth, or the prospective wife's Date of Birth, etc.

This is advanced Numerology that we take up at the end of the Practical Instruction, but I introduce it here so we can summarize the core elements of Matrix Analysis.

- Lines in the Matrix
- Stated and Vacant Trines in the Matrix
- Variations and Oppositions in the Matrix
- Patterns and Overlay Patterns in the Matrix

The area on Patterns has never been recorded in print except for clues left on the walls of an ancient temple of the Pythagoreans that was closed and sealed in the Catholic Persecutions of the Pagan Faiths after the Council of Trullo, 692 AD. (when the Court of the Holy Inquisition was founded)

In all, within this book you will find a remarkable amount of new, clear and well-researched information, as well as a wonderful and refreshingly simple way to read and interpret Numerical charts.

Book of Number: Practical

RECAP:

Let's look at some examples of converting a Date to a Matrix.

23/6/1876 1/12/1960 11/9/2017 19/9/2000 8/7/2013 5/5/1974

Get some practice resolving the Lines and Trines you find in each of these dates. The first example (23/6/1876) has a Vacant Trine on the 4/5/9 Aspect. Also the 1, 2, 3, 7 and 8 positions are all in balance. Can you find all the combinations of Three here?.

You have a 1/2/3 Line, 1/2/7 Trine, 1/2/8 Trine, 1/3/7 Trine, 1/3/8 Trine, 1/7/8 Trine, 2/3/7 Trine, 2/3/8 Trine and a 3/7/8 Trine.

A small clue. Start with the LOWEST number and work every combination you can moving up from that point. Then work on the ones from the second lowest, and so on.

Don't worry about interpretations. All we are concerned about right now is getting the idea of converting a date to a readable Pattern in the Matrix.

Shortly we will start working on incorporating the NAME as well and the Birth Date, and seeing how both of these resolve to two Matrix patterns, which we can then OVERLAY and gain a greater insight into the chart.

This ends the initial overview of the Matrix. Soon we will move to a more detailed study, but this will be done in sections, starting with a better understanding of Number (Noumenal) Weight.

Further Research

There is some information available in published books that is quite good. Marc Grunner and Robyn Stein are quality, well-researched authors and their books on Numerology are excellent and worthwhile reading. Dan Millman's "The Life you were Meant to Live" is the best source, by far, for Composite Number interpretations.

Cheiro's Book of Numbers, printed in 1932, remains one of the best sources for Chaldean Numerology and there are many areas the two systems overlap. This is an insightful book, and considered essential reading.

AUTHOR'S NOTES:

One of the things I feel it is important to mention is that some of you reading this material will find it strangely familiar. This is perhaps because you studied at one of the Pythagorean Universities in the past. For some 600 years, there were three types of university you could choose from: Pythagorean, Platonic, or Christian. The Pythagorean was considered the highest.

Pythagoras studied, in his early life, within the Orphic Mysteries. This taught that the Transmigration of Soul, or Reincarnation as we know it today, was a basic truth in Life. Your study of Number is not dependent on whether you accept this or otherwise, however, it is worthy of note that the real history of how reincarnation became a rejected principle in Western Thought is worthy of consideration.

Essentially, two factions (Monophysites versus the Origenists) in the Catholic Church fought over this concept for over a hundred years. Those who believed Jesus was the ascended and perfected man through a series of incarnations lost the battle, and all mention of reincarnation was removed from the Bible.

I have already had the privilege to teach some of the students who attended the school at Crotona. My task with these was not to teach so much as to remind them of the treasures from ages past that they can now collect. And maybe you will be another?

Book of Number: Practical

There is such a thing as Inner and Outer realities. We can cross between the two as easily as a child crosses from imagination to reality.

Perhaps in your study of Number, doors to your Inner Worlds will open for you. Insights will flow and you will hardly know where they came from. I know this happened for me. In the original writing of this book, I stopped many times and asked myself how I could make a claim of a particular thing.

Logic and my understanding of Number would lead me to a specific understanding, yet there was little in the way of historical evidence to back it up. Each time I received a significant answer to my doubts, leading me to some external evidence from the past, and even including visits on the Inner from Pythagoras himself.

On one occasion he opened the doors to his university, and there was no one inside. I wondered: Was this a message to leave it alone, that the time had passed? Or was it a message to re-fill the hall? To tell you the truth, I still don't know. What I do know is that when I woke up, and found myself back in the physical body, I had a strong desire to continue writing. So I did.

I trust that in this course you will find a few of the wonderful treasures from Ancient Times that I have condensed and brought to you in modern language. The process initially took some four years to complete, with significant revisions along the way. Regardless, it fell to me to compile this information and bring it to you.

There are still evolutions of the Matrix that can be expressed, such as shifting the Matrix into 3 dimensions using the 10, 11, 12 and 13/Zero. Perhaps in time and with computer graphics it will be right to re-open this aspect of Higher Numerology.

Since writing this course I have continued to evolve Pythagorean Teachings with the Harmonic Healing, as described by Plato. (This you will find at www.numberharmonics.org) In essence, this is a numerical chart put to music, and has received rave reviews from the public and also the professional tone healers who have used it.

NOUMENAL WEIGHT in the MATRIX

Let's spend a moment and go over the basics. The "weight" of numbers in the Matrix is very important. "Weight" is simply the number of times a Number appears, or is represented.

On the 13 April 1945 there are 2 x One and 2 x Four present in the date, with a Matrix that looks like this:

/		/
	/	
//	//	

13 / 4 / 1945 = 27 into NINE

On this day the greatest WEIGHT in the chart is on the One and the Four. Without a single weight being stronger than the others, the Dominant Number is less important. But there's an even "weight" on the 3, 5 and 9, so these form a Trine.

Also, we have four Vacant Numbers: 2, 6, 7 and 8. And so we have Vacant Trines between these numbers. Remember, go from lowest to highest, and it is easy to work out: 2/6/7, 2/6/8, 2/7/8 and 6/7/8.

The 1/5/9 Line has the greatest 'weight' so a 1/5/9 Line of Force is in effect, but notice there is the SAME WEIGHT on the 1/4/7 line. The fact that the line is incomplete (there is no 7) is relevant, but for now let's say that there's a 1/4/7 line as part of the interpretation.

Now we need to look at a NAME that goes with the Birth Date. Your Name is your primary identifier in this life, and it has a powerful effect over your destiny. We use the Magna Graecia Code, assign number to letter, and plot this into the matrix in the same way we do with the birth date.

Converting the NAME VALUE into the MATRIX

Obviously everyone has a name, and a goodly number of people have several names. The Name Value has a bearing on the birth date, and it is the main "modifier" of how the energy of the day you are born on affects you. To start with, let's go over how we create the Matrix from any given name.

Book of Number: Practical

Once more we need to refer to the Magna Graecia Code, and we reinsert it for easy reference:

A	B	C	D	E	F	G	H	I
J	K	L	M	N	O	P	Q	R
S	T	U	V	W	X	Y	Z	
1	2	3	4	5	6	7	8	9

Let's select a name and birth date and work it through till we find it's relevant matrix. As we have already looked at Richard Nixon, it's an easy one to start with. We will insert the Flow Chart already worked out, because all the information is listed there.

	9			1			9			1	3			9		6		38	11	2
R	I	C	H	A	R	D	M	I	L	H	A	U	S	N	I	X	O	N		
9		3	8		9	4	4		3	8			1	5		6		5	65	11	2
	Name Value								65 adds to 11. 38 + 11 = 49										49	22	4
	BIRTH					0	9	0	1	1	9	1	3							24	6
	DESTINY NUMBERS								49 + 24 = 73							37	46	10	1

Now we resolve the number "weight" in the name and the birth date into a matrix, after which we OVERLAY both of these to form a composite matrix with ALL weights in the name and date of birth.

/		//
///		

Birth Matrix

///	//	////
	//	//
///	//	

Name Matrix

////	//	//////
	//	//
//////	//	

Combined Matrix

Book of Number: Practical

I will list the aspects under each Matrix, but we do not have room to list their meanings. To make things simpler: If there is a Line of Force active, I write L.F. after the numbers associated with it. If there is a BALANCED Line active, I will write L.B. When a Trine is present I put simply T, and a Vacant Trine is V.T. An Opposition is OPP. And Cyclic Trines (which we will discuss later) are C.T.

We also have a lot of PATTERNS in Nixon's chart, but these come later. We will look at these advanced Aspects in due course.

/		//
///		

Birth Matrix

1-5-9 L.F.

2-5-7 L.B

4-5-6 L.B

1-3-9 C.T

Vacant Trines:

2-4-5, 2-4-6, 2-4-7, 2-4-8, 2-5-6, 2,5,7, 2-6-7, 2-6-8, 4-5-7, 4-5-8, 4-6-7, 4-6-8, 4-7-8, 5-6-7, 5-6-8, 6-7-8

Plus THREE major Patterns

Dominant ONE

///	//	/////
	//	//
///	//	

Name Matrix

1-5-9 L.F.

3-6-9 L.F.

4-5-6 L.B.

4-5-8 T

4-6-8 T

5-6-8 T

2-7 OPP

"V" PATTERN

Dominant NINE

Surprised at how much there is in here? A simple thing like a Date of Birth and a Name can create a lot of information.

////	//	////////
	//	//
/////	//	

Combined Matrix

1-5-9 L.F.

4-5-6 L.B.

4-5-8 T

4-6-8 T

5-6-8 T

2-7 OPP

Dominant NINE

Book of Number: Practical

Can you see how the "weight" of each number combines to create Aspects? What's more, there are many aspects that REPEAT themselves. Just as we use the weight of Numbers in a chart to create an Aspect, a repeating Aspect creates it own "weight".

The repeating Aspects common to all three matrix charts are the 1-5-9 Line of Force, the 4-5-6 Line of Balance, the 4-5-8 T, 4-6-8 T and 5-6-8 T (trines) repeating in the name, birth and combined Matrix. These repeating aspects will be the defining forces at work in Nixon's chart. In all, it adds up to a driven man, a man who felt strong forces at work behind his thoughts and feelings since he was a child.

The "push" these aspects give is very significant. He would have felt he was chosen for an important role, and regardless of what the aspects might mean, so many repeating aspects lining up for the Birth, Name and Overlay Matrix will set the stage for spectacular success, or total failure. Nixon managed to achieve both.

Side Bar: The 1-3-9 "Cyclic Trine" in the Birth Date exists because the numbers have a weight that goes up evenly. The 3 has a weight of 1, the 9 has a weight of 2, and the 1 has a weight of 3. Read it in Interpretations Book as a normal Trine. Without going too far into it, we can also run from any Vacant position, to a One Weight, to a Two Weight, and get a myriad of Cyclic Trines as well.

Needless to say, this is an EXTREMELY intense chart with a tremendous degree of complicated and interlocking Aspects. You are welcome to go through the interpretations for each Aspect, and see what you can make of it, but the main point is that we have used the WEIGHT of NUMBER to find the ASPECT in the Matrix.

In the coming pages, we will start to look at each major Aspect and how we determine them, but for now we want to grasp the simple fact that the WEIGHT of a Number is the amount of times it is represented in the birth or name of the individual. The WEIGHT of Number determines the Aspects, not the numbers themselves.

Book of Number: Practical

A quick overview of the repeating Aspects in Nixon's Chart:

1-5-9 Line of Force

This aspect indicates a need for success. It does not determine actual success, merely the need for it, often combined with the subsequent fear of failure that this might not be so.

4-5-6 Line of Balance

This is a curious line, for it crosses many boundaries. It indicates business, also the home life, and yet also the sense of intuition we all possess but rarely utilize. Most of all this Line of Force indicates the Will to Persevere. Because of this, the native with this Aspect often develops a strong sense of his/her own worth. This sense of personal value is necessary in the long run, but this is often a completely self-inflated (or deflated!) opinion of self.

4-5-8 Trine

If the person with this aspect is of a higher mind and not needing so much in the way of material goods, this aspect is good. However, if they are materially minded with their goals and aspirations, bad luck may well seem to dog their every move. Spiritual Purpose must be found if peace is to settle in the heart.

4-6-8 Trine

Self-Employment is highlighted. This is a Money Trine, so called because the individual with this aspect is very likely to make a lot of money in their lives. If it is not actual cash, it will be a wealth of some sort, even a spiritual wealth of wisdom and knowledge, which perhaps is the greatest of the riches we can earn, for this we can take with us past the grave.

5-6-8 Trine

The worst scenario here is that this Soul will refuse to recognize the need for patience, and barge on regardless, never finding any pivot or base in their lives, and therefore accomplishing little. The sense of frustration from this can be crushing. Sometimes the very need for results that these people can feel is the very thing that prevents results from occurring.

The actual chart would run for over 60 pages and we have no room in our book to cover it, but this gives you some sort of idea.

Book of Number: Practical

Weight of Number Summary

Often the new student gets confused with the terms such as "weight" and "aspect". So once more, any given Date of Birth gives us a series of numbers.

- All numbers that have the same level of representation, or "weight" are in a relationship to each other.
- Vacant Numbers ALL SHARE THE SAME WEIGHT (Zero). All Vacant numbers have a relationship. The fact there IS no representation of a number can make it MORE relevant.
- To form an "aspect" we need three or more numbers of "equal weight", with odd exceptions like Oppositions, etc.

HOMEWORK:

Form a Matrix and work out the basic Matrix Patterns for the following dates:

31 Dec 1976

17 April 1862

14 Nov 1951

1 Aug 2003

If you can work out some basic Aspects for the above examples, write them beside the Matrix you have created, and look them up.

When Finished this section, GO TO: <u>Lines in the Matrix</u>

Lines in the Matrix

One of the common teachings in Numerology is the Matrix. It looks like the "Noughts and Crosses" pattern people use. You will find the Matrix in many Numerology books. It is used to find Aspects from the Date of Birth and the Name. It is used, but the understanding of it it is incomplete. In this book I will attempt to convey a far more comprehensive view of the Matrix.

I advise that we also have areas within the study of the Matrix not yet covered in the modern books. In fact, the last time information about Trines was in print was in a Rosicrucian publication in the early 1800's. I was only given a brief glance through this book, but I was told by an old Rosicrucian (after he read my material) that what I was doing was the same. In fact, he assumed I must have been a "high up" member to have access to such knowledge.

I am not a highly-ranked mystic in any organization. I simply applied Pythagorean Logic and came to the natural conclusions. Some time after talking to my Rosicrucian friend, I received a curious confirmation I was on the right track. The patterns I worked with were found inscribed in a 6th century temple to Pythagoras. The temple had been rediscovered in the early 1990's.

The core principles of the Pythagorean Teachings follow clear logic paths. Simple application of Pythagorean thinking will unveil the truth. If you can learn to walk in the great man's way of thinking, all things in this course will become self-evident.

I know this to be truth, because every time a student really starts tuning into the realities that lie under the words, they write to me about aspects of advanced Numerology that "just occurred" to them, or that they saw in a dream. It happens repeatedly.

That is how it is. The Pythagorean thought forms follow particular and peculiar logistics of the heart. The natural logic forms inescapable conclusions, even when an answer is derived from a limited source of information. In Mathematics, we call this Algebra.

Book of Number: Practical

LINES in the MATRIX: What they are.

Let us revise the Number Positions within the Matrix. Having a consistent pattern is very important. The positions are below, and these simply associate a "place" for a number position.

3	6	9
2	5	8
1	4	7

The Number Positions

The represented Numbers within any chart are recorded into the "space" where that number is represented.

If you were born on the 1 Feb 1987, then you have: 2 x One, 1 x Two, 1 x Seven, 1 x Eight, and 1 x Nine present in your chart.

		/
/		/
//		/

Normally we write the Number representation as STROKES: This is because when we get to complex Matrix patterns, there can be too many numbers in a box for them to fit. Strokes are neater.

		/
/		/
//		/

This forms the following relationships:

Dominant One, Incomplete 1-2-3, 1-5-9, 1-4-7 LF

2-7-8 T, 2-7-9 T, 2-8-9 T, 7-8-9 LB

3-4-5 VT, 3-4-6 VT, 3-5-6 VT, with the the 4-5-6 Vacant Line, and the 7-8-9 Line of Balance.

There are many number relationships in this date, but for now we will only be looking at the LINES in the Matrix. In particular, the "simple" stated Line of Force, but also the Incomplete Line of Force on the 1-2-3, 1-5-9 and 1-4-7 axis, the Line of Balance on the 7-8-9 axis, and the VACANT Line of Balance on the 4-5-6 axis.

As we progress through these early stages, know that already you have surpassed the depth of knowledge found in the majority of books in print. This book represents a year of full time study, so take the time to cover these basics carefully. And practice on your friends. Experience is the truest, most reliable teacher.

Book of Number: Practical

Lines in the Matrix denote energy flowing in a client's life. They are like a brand that leads the energy on set paths. A person with a 7-8-9 Line of Altruism will have altruistic tendencies, for example.

In almost every Matrix Chart we will find LINES of energy that come into play in accordance to the date or name of an individual.

There are EIGHT Lines Possible in the Matrix. These are:

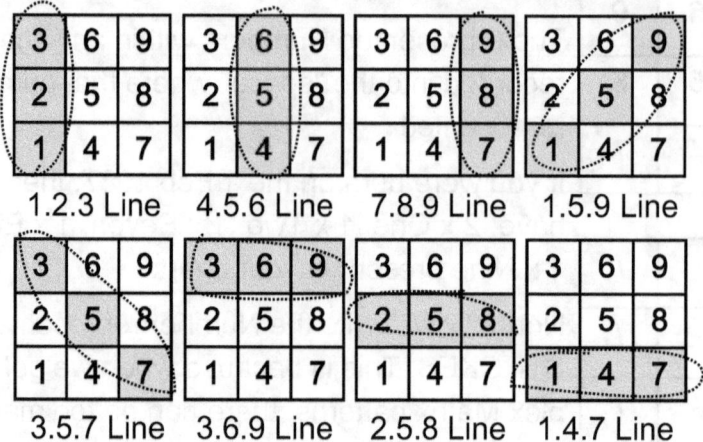

1.2.3 Line   4.5.6 Line   7.8.9 Line   1.5.9 Line

3.5.7 Line   3.6.9 Line   2.5.8 Line   1.4.7 Line

A Line is determined from specific characteristics based on the WEIGHT OF NUMBERS REPRESENTED IN THAT LINE. We have already described this in brief but let's go over it again.

LINES in the MATRIX: Determining Weight

"Weight" is everything. Before we will be able to grasp and apply ANY of the lines, trines and patterns that can occur in a Numerical Chart we need to have this firmly fixed in our minds.

Let's take an example. The date of the 17 May 1956 gives a good indication of a simple Line in the Matrix. (Pictured)

Clearly the greatest "weight" here is on the 1.5.9 axis. This is the 1.5.9 Line of Force. This is the Line of Success, and so the notion of striving for success will be important to this person. There are other aspects, but this is the most obvious.

Book of Number: Practical

13 April 1945 = 27 into NINE

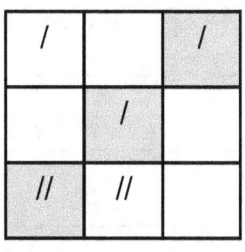

On this day the **greatest weight** of individual numbers in the chart is on the **One** and the **Four**, equally. This means we look at these to include them in the chart reading. But as far as a LINE goes, the Greatest Weight must be over a LINE, not just a number.

As stated, when we are looking to work out a LINE we need to look at the LINE or LINES that have the Greatest Weight. And here we have an interesting scenario. A thing called an INCOMPLETE Line.

The 1-4-7 Line has an overall WEIGHT of four strokes, but the Number 7 is VACANT making the Line Incomplete

The 1-5-9 Line has the SAME overall Weight of Four Strokes, but this line is COMPLETE. This is the most prevalent Line in this Matrix, because it is complete. The 1-4-7 Line has the same weight, but as it is not complete, it generally has less influence.

Note that the 1-2-3 Line has an overall weight of THREE. In this case it is DISCARDED as an influence in this chart. So too does the 4-5-6 Line have a weight of THREE, and thus is not relevant.

The Main Line, the 1-5-9 Line, is known as a Line of FORCE. The Second Line is in a different category. It is an Incomplete Line to start with, but it also has both represented Numbers in EQUAL Balance. It's one of those curious Aspects that can come into play later in the chart. Note too, the 3 and 5 have the same weight, and if there were a weight on the 7, there would be a Line of Balance. If the energy of the SEVEN is enhanced, everything changes.

So, we have a definite Aspect on the 1-5-9 Line, and a weaker Aspect with the 1-4-7 Line. The Vacant Seven MAY be important. The Vacant Trines, the implied "cross" Pattern on the 1-5-9/3-5-7 line, all indicate this Vacant Seven may become something of a focus in the chart. You have to go through all the variables to resolve a likely direction for the chart. It's all a moveable feast, and nothing is nailed down until ALL aspects are considered.

MATRIX for 13 / 06 / 1945

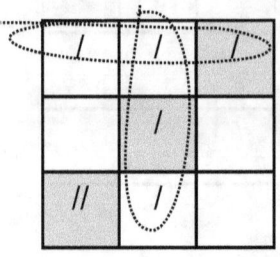

If the Date was **13 June 1945** it would all be very different, You can see the Line of Force on the 1-5-9 Line, but there are TWO lines that both have Equal Weight. Equal weight on the 4-5-6 and 3-6-9 Lines make them Lines of BALANCE. Notice they form a "T" shape? This is called a "T" Pattern, and we look at this later in the book.

We still have the GREATEST WEIGHT on the 1-5-9 Line of FORCE, but now we have several other lines that, while not Lines of FORCE, have every number equally represented.

These Lines of BALANCE can be extremely powerful. Like all things in Numerology, it is a shifting tide of importance as to how much influence any particular Aspect will have. Everything always depends on everything else in the chart, but one thing is certain, as you get used to the shifting sands, you will find a rock solid base underpinning it all.

For now we have TWO types of Line in the Matrix: The Line that simply has the strongest representation of Number (which we call the Line of Force), and the Line that has every number equally distributed, (which is called a Line of BALANCE).

The above Matrix has a 1-5-9 Line of Force, plus a 3-6-9 and 4-5-6 Line of Balance. These are called "Aspects". Please keep in mind this concept of "strongest" weight and "equal" weight both sharing significance. This is a core principle with the Pythagorean Matrix.

We will include ALL of the Aspects as well as their interpretations in the Book of Interpretations. (Book II) But of course, before this is of any use to you, we first need to understand how to develop and qualify what aspects apply in any given chart.

As you get familiar with all of the many and various possibilities, you will be amazed at how apparently random Aspects all add up to a very complete understanding of the person you are looking at. It's always a surprise, and I look at every chart as a puzzle to solve.

Book of Number: Practical

Let's look at another example: 12 Jan 1855 (12 / 1 / 1855)

1+2+1+1+8+5+5 = 23 into 5. Here the Greatest Weight is once more along the 1-5-9 Line, with a weight of Five strokes, but this Line is incomplete!

There is no NINE. Here we have a new element. The chart has an Incomplete Line of Force on the 1-5-9 axis, but the strongest force is really the VACANT Line along the 3-6-9 axis.

The 3-6-9 Line in the VACANT position. Even though there is nothing there, all number positions share an EQUAL WEIGHT. It may be all VACANT, but it shares the SAME WEIGHT of ZERO. This means we have an energy on the 3-6-9 VACANT LINE.

Here is the tricky bit. The FULL line, no matter what type (Force, Balance or Vacant) always has more strength than any Incomplete Line. And so in this Chart, the 3-6-9 Vacant Line carries the greatest influence, even though it isn't actually there!

If the energy of the NINE was introduced, everything changes. This can happen if you marry someone strong in the Nine, for instance.

Note that the 2-5-8 Line appears to be a Line of Force, but it only has a representation of FOUR STROKES, compared to the Incomplete Line with Five. The 2-5-8 Line does not count here.

SO! We have THREE types of Line. The Line of FORCE, the Line of BALANCE, and the VACANT Line. Let's recap.

Once more with feeling:

- A Line of FORCE is a line in the Matrix that has the GREATEST WEIGHT
- A Line of BALANCE is a Line in the Matrix that has EQUAL WEIGHT
- A VACANT Line is a Line where all number positions are Vacant.
- An INCOMPLETE Line is a Line with a Vacant Number.

Book of Number: Practical

Let's alter this last Matrix a little: 2 Jan 1855

Here we find the Line of Force along the 1-5-9 Line is now an Incomplete Line of Balance, while the 2-5-8 Line now carries the Line of Force. The Vacant 3-6-9 Line is still present, but now we have THREE active Aspects to consider when reading this chart.

Curiously, I could find only one person of note with this birth date, the tennis player and Wimbelton champion, Frank Hadow. He is the only male tennis champion to have never lost a set at Wimbelton, possibly because he only played there once. (True)

He never went back, calling tennis a "sissy game". He far preferred hunting big game in Africa, and is registered in the 1928 Roland Ward's "Records of Big Game" with many trophies to his name. His father was chairman of the P&O line.

It is this crazy combination of his Harrow Education, this Wimbelton Champion and big game hunter earned an income running a coffee plantation in Ceylon! This crazy eclectic mix makes an interesting subject to match against the Birth Matrix.

- 1-5-9 Line of Success, incomplete. He was a Wimbelton Champion who never bothered to return to defend the title.
- 2-5-8 Line of Force. He was an adventuresome and intrepid hunter in what was once wildest Africa.
- Vacant 3-6-9 Line of the Mind. This is the man who, though he considered tennis a "sissy game", invented the Lob as a way to break volley service. It was a game changing innovation.

A very curious fellow indeed.

This "what if" game of adding or removing a number to change the weight of a Matrix, and seeing how it affects things has a very useful purpose. As one example, we often get two people who are considering marriage coming in to have a numerical chart created. Here we OVERLAY the birth matrix of the husband and wife to be, and see what new forms are created in the Matrix.

It is extraordinary what can be discovered with such a simple exercise. The notion of compatibility, likely issues that will crop up, and positive/negative aspects can be easily seen and discussed. (We cover this in the Overlay Matrix section, page 117)

Book of Number: Practical

General Discussion

One of the problems of trying to understand Numerology from a book is that the words can get in the way. I can sit down with a student and in just three hours teach them how to compile a Numerical Chart. Yet when you have no teacher at hand, it takes weeks to "get it". It is difficult sorting through everything without someone on hand. However, the advantage of this book is that it is a permanent record. We are creating, or recreating as the case may be, the pattern for many to follow in the future.

The concept of a Line in the Matrix is not a particularly difficult idea to get. Once you grasp the simplicity of how "weight" creates Aspects, the other Aspects that come about because of "weight" "balance" or "vacancy" in the Matrix will be easier to spot.

Lines in the Matrix: VARIATIONS

Now we get into the subtler parts to understand. You may have already noticed, in Lines of Force, one number will have more "weight" that the others? This is what is called an "Accent" on a particular Line. If on any given Line there is a number that weighs more than the other numbers on that line, it is given the position of an ACCENT. In the Book of Interpretations we give the meaning for each Line in the Matrix, and we offer an addendum interpretation for all possible accents as, and when, they occur.

In a VACANT line there can be no Accent. In an Incomplete Line of Force or Balance the "Accent" is usually on the vacant position.

In the Line of Force, the Accent is like the energy is breathing OUT at that point, and on the Incomplete Line of Balance, it is like the chart is breathing IN this energy

Of course, it can also go the other way! That's the curious thing about numbers, their effect on the individual will adjust and mutate as the person's consciousness alters.

Book of Number: Practical

HOMEWORK Exercise for PART ONE

In the Matrix Patterns Below, write down the LINES that are Aspected and which have significance. Interpretation is NOT necessary. Just work out what Lines are valid and part of the reading for that Date.

Exercise One

		/
	//	
//	///	

Exercise Two

/	//	/
	/	
//	//	

Exercise Three

/		/
/	/	
//	//	/

Exercise Four

/		/
/	/	/
/	//	/

Closing Comment

It is very important to grasp how an Aspect is created through the weight of number in the Matrix. As you go through the above homework, try and take into consideration how things might change if any given number were stronger or weaker in weight.

All this becomes extremely relevant when going into the deeper aspects of the Matrix, and in particular when we look to working out how people's energy will combine in relationships, etc.

The next stage of our study is: **Trines in the Matrix**

"Salt is born of the purest parents: the sun and the sea"

Pythagoras

TRINES

There is geometry in the humming of the strings, there is music in the spacing of the spheres.

Pythagoras

The above quote is a perfect way to introduce the principle of Pythagorean Trines. In music, you need three harmonious notes to create a chord. Whenever you create two notes in resonance with each other, a third will manifest. It is a simple principle of physics, and you hear it as a harmonic, or overtone.

So too does the Law of Three holds true in an individual's Number Chart. We are always looking for a combination of Three.

Whenever you have three points of resonance, you create a chord, a specific energy that is defined. For those with the spiritual ears to hear, you can "hear" the music in a person's chart as clearly as I can hear people having a conversation beside me.

The knowledge of these Pythagorean Trines is almost unknown.

The last reference I could find was in an 18th century book I was briefly shown by a Rosicrucian. The patterns for trine do occur in a temple to Pythagoras that was unearthed in Rome in 1993, and so we have some sort of historical basis for this.

But the proof is in the pudding. As you practise and understand how powerful the Trines are, you will simply be amazed. They are so quick and easy to find in a person's numerical chart, and in minutes you can be gaining a clear insight to questions a person may be asking.

This next study on Trines is core to understanding Pythagorean Numerology.

Book of Number: Practical

TRINES in the MATRIX

Now that we have begun to understand how to resolve and grasp the Aspect of a LINE in a Matrix, we need to start expanding and discover the other Aspects.

In this area we are looking at TRINES in the Matrix. Grasp the power of Trines and you will leave your friends stunned and amazed at their extraordinary accuracy.

A Trine (except in an odd circumstance known as a Cyclic Trine) is in effect the same as the LINE OF BALANCE or VACANT LINE, but in a Triangle Pattern, not a straight line.

The same rules apply. Any combination of 3 elements of EQUAL WEIGHT create a TRIANGLE, or what we call a Trine.

A: We have STATED TRINES, which come about whenever we have THREE NUMBERS (not on an axis) with the SAME REPRESENTATION. (Equal Weight)

B: We have VACANT TRINES, which come about when we have THREE VACANT Numbers (not on an axis) in the Matrix.

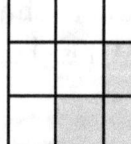

19 May 1967   4-6-7 Trine

On the **19/5/1967** we have a 5-6-7 Trine in the STATED position, while the VACANT 2, 3, 4 and 8 create the 2-3-4, 2-3-8, 2-4-8 and 3-4-8 VACANT TRINES

23 May 1962   4-7-8 Trine

On the **23/5/1962** we have a VACANT 4-7-8 TRINE. We also have many STATED TRINES: 1-3-5, 1-3-6, 1-3-9, 1-5-6, 3-5-6, 3-5-9, 5-6-9. We also have the 1-2-3 Line of Force, with the 1-4-9 and 3-6-9 Lines of Balance

C: We must also consider that if a VACANT TRINE is CROSSED by any aspect, it's effect is weakened and sometimes cancelled.

Book of Number: Practical

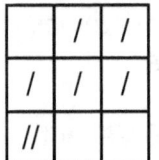 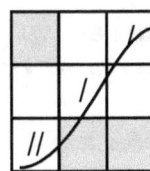 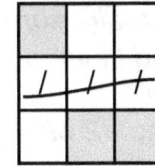

On the 12 / 5 / 1986 there is a Vacant 3-4-7 Trine crossed by a 1-5-9 Line of Force and a 2-5-8 Line of Balance. The Vacant Trine is weak here.

In the above example a Vacant Trine is present, but as the 2-5-8 Line of Balance and the 1-5-9 Line of Force cross it, this weakens the effect of the Trine. But this does not discount the influence. Different situations can "wake" up Aspects like this.

The energy is just sleeping, in a sense. In circumstances where the 3-4-7 numbers occur in a date, or if the person affected by the Trine meets another person who has this Trine strongly evident, then the energy of this Vacant Trine will surface more readily.

A Trine, or any Aspect, that is normally "suppressed" by the other Aspects in a chart can be awoken in several ways. Typically a person who has a "suppressed" 3-4-7 Trine would find its effect is getting stronger coming up to the date 3 July 2004. (pictured) Clearly the Trine is stronger on this date.

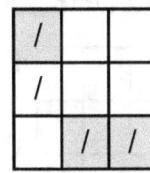
3 July 2004

The overall rule of Numerology is very simple. ALL NUMBERS INTERACT WITH THE ENERGY AROUND THEM. A suppressed aspect can become ascendant and extremely powerful when a date, a person or a situation brings it into focus.

We generally have a number of Trines in any given chart. They are all looked at individually, but are interpreted in much the same way as a Tarot card reader looks at a number of cards.

Each Trine has its own meaning, but it is in combination with other Trines that the overall effect is made known. In many ways, the different Trines represent "voices" in a choir, which can be in either harmony or disharmony. What this means is simple. Every chart forms a unique picture, or song, for each individual.

Just as specific days can "call in" the energy of a Trine if the Trine is aspected on that day, similarly meeting a person strong in a specific Aspect can "awaken" that Aspect within ourselves. This is especially marked if someone marries a person, and the "Overlay" Matrix between the two persons highlights any Trine or Aspect from the other person's Natal Chart.

Book of Number: Practical

Let's look at other options, and make sure we can work out exactly what it is that creates Trines and Lines on any given date.

On a day such as the *12 May 1963* the 4-7-8 Vacant Trine is clearly active. (*The Vacant 4-7-8 Trine is a powerful influence. It could not occur during the 1700's and 1800's but it is common from the 1900's on*)

The above Chart gives us: Dominant ONE
1-2-3 and 1-5-9 Lines of Force and 3-6-9 Line of Balance
4-7-8 Vacant Trine (very strong - nothing crossing it)
2-3-5, 2-3-6, 2-3-9, 2-5-6, 2-5-9, 2-6-9, 3-5-6, 3-5-9, 5-6-9 Trines

The Date *23 August 2012* gives us:

Dominant TWO, 1-2-3 Line of Force, 4-5-6 Vacant Line, 1-3-8 Stated Trine, 4-5-7, 4-5-9, 4-6-7, 4-6-9, 4-7-9, 5-6-7, 5-6-9, 6-7-9 Vacant Trines

The Date *7 October 1986* gives us:

Dominant ONE, 1-5-9 and 1-4-7 Incomplete Lines of Force, 3-5-7 Vacant Line, 4-6-8, 4-6-9, 4-8-9 and 6-8-9 Stated Trines, 2-3-5, 2-3-7 and 2-5-7 Vacant Trines

Let's add a NAME to this Date: (*Susan Peters* = 1, 3, 1, 1, 5, 7, 5, 2, 5, 9, 1) which forms a Matrix with a clear 1-5-9 Line of Force. There is also a VACANT trine to match the 4-6-8 Stated Trine in the date (7 Oct 1986) and the 2-3-7, 2-3-9, 2-7-9 and 3-7-9 Trines.

Now we ADD both Matrix charts together.

Simply put all the weights off number from BOTH charts into a single Matrix. The 1-5-9 Line still is very strong, and the 4-6-8 Trine is still evident.

There are many other Trines in the Overlay Matrix. There are the 2-3-6 and 4-7-8 Stated Trines, for example. There is also an extremely powerful 2-4-6-8 Cross Pattern, but the REPEATING Aspects are the 1-5-9 Line and 4-6-8 Trine. Because they repeat, they have added importance.

So we have gone through the process, isolated Aspects, done an Overlay Matrix to find Dominant Aspects. We have all the information, but how do we interpret this? This is always the elephant in the room, but let's try to offer some suggestions below.

Susan Peters, born 7 Oct 1986

Note the REPEATING 4-6-8 TRINE and the REPEATING 1-5-9 LINE of FORCE are the Dominant Aspects for the chart.

When you see REPEATING ASPECTS in both the Name and Date of Birth, it is highly significant. The 4-6-8 Trine is often seen in people who work for themselves in some way, and the Line of Success indicates the desire to move upwards. Logically, these two Aspects indicate that the person would be happiest in their own business.

The OVERLAY MATRIX tells us the "Destiny" if you will. What does it all add up to? In this case there are only four strong aspects, the Line of Force, the flanking Trines (2-3-6 and 4-7-8) and the Square Pattern with the 2-4-6-8. (See "Patterns in the Matrix")

In simple terms this is the sort of chart you would see in a fairly driven person. It suits an evangelist, someone out driving a greater cause, or a person prepared to cope with much to achieve a goal.

But what is the reality? So often a person will reverse their natural flow, and you have to decide where they are internally. (See "The Four Querent Modes" in Book III - Client Psychology) You may find Sue is a sullen, withdrawn individual who seems almost "mouse-like". You may well find these patterns in a librarian, someone surrounded with great and noble deeds, yet who remains cloistered in a safe house, not risking failure by seeking to achieve too much.

Getting the idea? Just because as Aspect suggests a significant something does not in any way mean that the person will achieve this. In truth, the stronger the aspects, the less a person tends to be able to deal with the energy, and the more withdrawn they are.

You need to adjust every single reading to suit the situation.

Book of Number: Practical

Discovering the Truth of Numerology

In all we have covered so far, we have essentially been learning how to FIND THE ASPECT. Do not be concerned overmuch with interpretation at this point, that comes with practice. What is essential is to accurately and quickly determine what Aspects are at work in a name and date of birth.

No written body of work can give you experience. All I can do is point you towards the salient facts, and the general interpretation of Aspects, and in time you will work out how it all fits. Practice on friends and relatives until you feel it starting to gel.

At some point it will go "CLICK!" You will have the "Ah-Ha" moment Oprah speaks of, and it will start to make sense.

It happened with myself after a few years of playing with all this. I was reading charts to impress some girls in a coffee shop when a young German male of around 24 years came up, and said, "So, you think you can fool people with this, hey?"

What could I say? The gauntlet had been thrown down, and it was clearly a challenge. "Did you want me to do an analysis on yourself, my friend?" I asked. The girls all looked at the German.

He laughed. "Sure, but I have had four different names since birth."

"You changed your name four times?" I asked.

"My name was changed through different circumstances, moving countries, my mother getting re-married, that sort of thing," he answered. He was the typical sceptic, confident in his disbelief.

I always preferred hard-nosed people to those who like to believe everything. So for me, this was fun. I was the one who was surprised, however, when the "Ah Ha" moment came. Something opened up as I went through all the changing patterns that came from the different names. I could see quite easily and clearly the effect the different Aspects would be having with every name change, and what sort of emotional and mental difficulties could likely come about as a result.

Book of Number: Practical

I was even able to predict the approximate time of each name change, which surprised me even more. It was simply how things added up. I spent over FOUR HOURS reading this fellow's chart, using napkins and whatever came to hand in the coffee shop.

It seemed like 20 minutes, we were all so engrossed. The ENTIRE TIME he sat there utterly stone-faced, giving absolutely no indication if anything I said was correct or otherwise. In the end, I had exhausted all the likely scenarios, and said "Well, how was that?"

The flood gates opened. He shook his head, and looked stunned. He just ranted. "It is not possible. I gave you NO indication, I know! It is utterly impossible. It is NOT POSSIBLE you could have known every detail of my life! Even the years you gave when my names changed were accurate, and everything you said about how I thought and felt was absolutely correct. It is not possible. This is simply NOT POSSIBLE! Who gave you this information?"

"You did." Even though I was probably more surprised than the German, I looked at the fellow quite candidly, and said, "You gave me the numerical facts. I just read the information you gave to me."

It was only then I realised that the cafe had filled, and we were surrounded by people, 20 deep, all wildly applauding this apparent miracle. We had started in the afternoon, and it was now dark. Time and space itself had appeared to have collapsed

That my friends, that exact point in time, was when I realised I held a very great truth. I was more surprised by this outcome than our young German. I had been taking pot shots, and had just guessed at likely outcomes, based on what seemed common sense, and on my understanding of what each number combination meant.

To have a total disbeliever who gave no clues or signals to totally confirm the accuracy of what I was playing with told me a simple undeniable truth. I needed to get more serious. I had to understand how the Pythagoreans used Number to understand reality.

And the result, some 33 years later, is the book you now hold.

Book of Number: Practical

The Harmonic Principles of Number

One of the great secrets that evolved in my period of study is that the Trines relate directly to harmonic signatures. They have a specific "tone" that can be converted into musical sequences, and played to a person. For now, it is not necessary for you to have a musical knowledge, but if you do, treat each Trine as an interval structure in music, and HEAR what it sounds like.

A 1-6-7 Trine, for instance can be played as the Tonic, Sixth, and Seventh note of any scale. Further, as all music modulates between Major and Minor, you can play the Tonic, Flat Sixth, Flat Seventh. This tells the story of the Trine in the "minor" or in-breathing aspect. (Obviously "8" refers to the Tonic one octave higher, and "9" refers to the "9th", or the Second, one octave higher)

We group each Trine in a cluster relating to its structure. Please note that each specific Trine in the "Minor" group does not directly mean a Minor chord, or a Major trine to a Major Chord, etc. There is a relationship, but it is not as specific as this.

For the musicians reading this, the Birth Number represents the Tonic Note of the Individual. A = 1, Bb = 2, and so on. A person with a FOUR birth number is in the Key of "C".

If they have a 1-4-5 Trine present, this relates to the 1st, 4th and 5th notes in the "C" scale. (C, F and G). The relationship here is very simple and direct. Your Birth Date gives the Tonic Note and the numbers in the Trine are directly linked to the Interval Structure of the scale relating to that note.

Modal Theory is applicable, and indeed, gives clear specifics as to the "moods" the individual will experience with the Aspects shown in the chart.

Information is available on line at: www.numberharmonics.org

Book of Number: Practical

Pictorial Summary of Trines

In this next section we will be giving every type of Trine that exists in the Matrix as a graphic. The reason is simple, it is easy to confuse numbers, but the picture tells you exactly what it is.

As always, the interpretations for all these are in the Book of Interpretations. The way we use this next section is to use a friend's chart, isolate likely Trines, and just get used to spotting them in the Matrix.

In no time at all, this all becomes second nature, but for now keep the reference to hand and double check each aspect you find to make sure it is here.

You will also note a famous person beside each Group of Trines. Again this is simply a clue to show you how a Trine occurs in an actual Birth Matrix.

Do not be concerned with the names of the Trine Groups. This simply describes a type, and makes it easier to reference when looking up interpretations. Take your time, use the charts of friends and relatives, and get used just finding the relevant Trines.

We list these groups in a pictorial context. In order to make it quick and easy reference the shaded area relates to the relevant Trine.

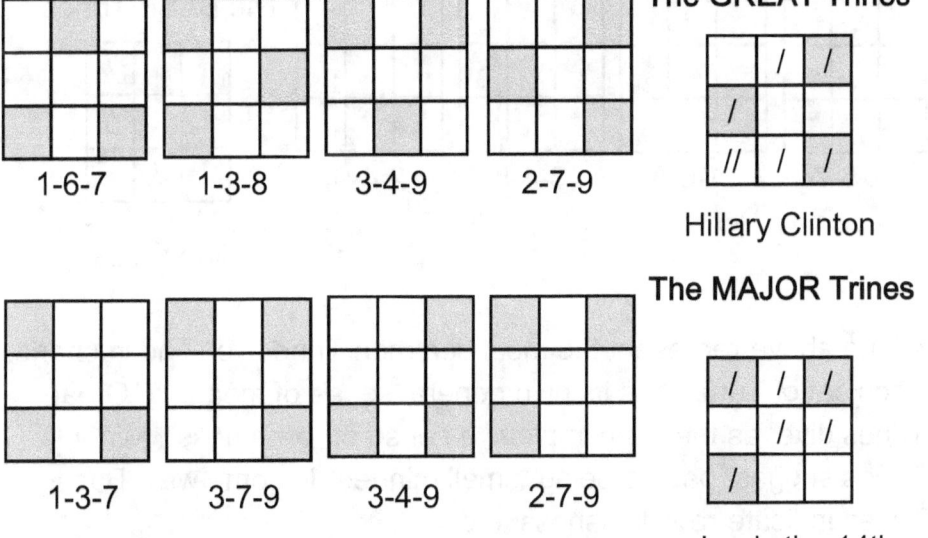

The GREAT Trines

1-6-7   1-3-8   3-4-9   2-7-9

Hillary Clinton

The MAJOR Trines

1-3-7   3-7-9   3-4-9   2-7-9

Louis the 14th

Book of Number: Practical

The MINOR Trines

1-2-4   2-3-6   6-8-9   4-7-8

4-5-6   2-4-5   2-5-6   5-6-8

4-5-6   4-5-7   5-7-8   5-8-9

5-6-9   3-5-6   2-3-5   1-2-5

Louis the 16th

(Note the large number of Minor Trines in the Birth Date of this unfortunate monarch)

The BASE Trines

2-6-7   1-6-8   3-4-8   2-4-9

Adolf Hitler

All the above represent the most common Trines you find in charts. Each set of Trines has its own general sense of meaning. Great Trines give, as the word implies, a sense of "greatness". Minor Trines suggest people being "small minded" in some way. Base Trines indicate rebelliousness, etc.

Book of Number: Practical

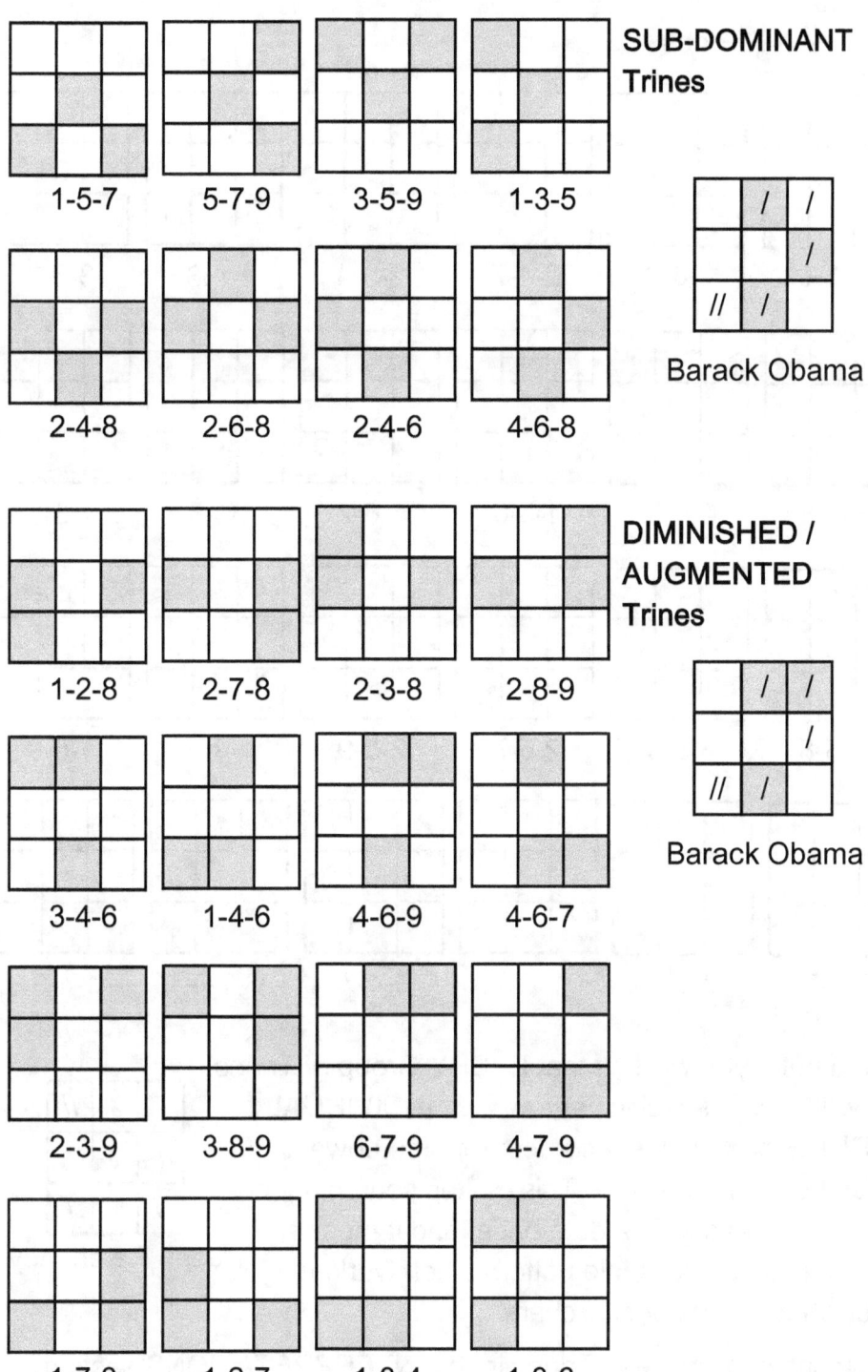

Book of Number: Practical

VARIANT Trines

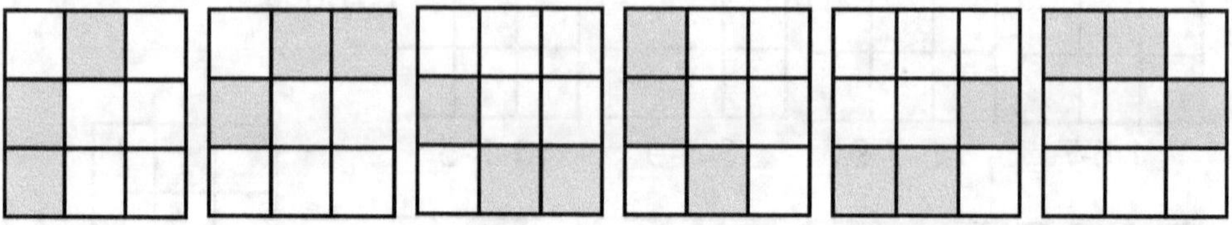

| 1-2-6 | 2-6-9 | 2-4-7 | 2-3-4 | 1-4-8 | 3-6-8 |

| 6-7-8 | 4-8-9 | 1-5-6 | 5-6-7 | 3-4-5 | 4-5-9 |

| 1-5-8 | 3-5-8 | 2-5-7 | 2-5-9 | 1-8-9 | 1-6-9 |

| 3-6-7 | 2-3-7 | 1-2-9 | 3-4-7 | 3-7-8 | 1-4-9 |

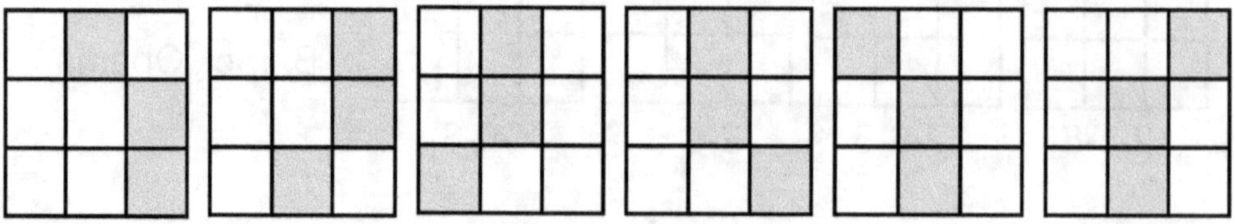

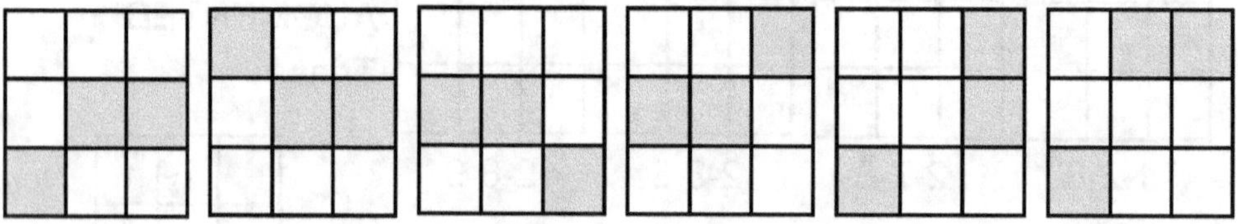

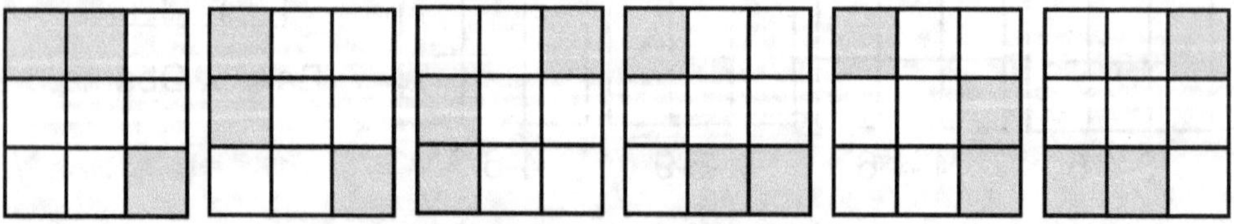

As a note, you will see that EVERY Group of Trines is written is a specific pattern. ALL INDIVIDUAL TRINES are always recorded from the Lowest Number to the Highest. This makes searching for them a lot easier in a data base, and it means you can follow a simple pattern when working out what is in a specific chart.

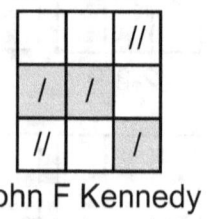

John F Kennedy

You can search these Trines in the INTERPRETATIONS section. They are grouped according to TYPE (Great, Base, Minor, etc.)

GENERAL INFORMATION: TRINES

The Spiritual Law of Three has been axiomatic since ancient times.

Pythagoras described the Three as the "Perfect Number" and makes it a symbol of Deity. The world was supposed to be under the rule of three Gods, viz. Jupiter (heaven), Neptune (sea), and Pluto (Hades).

Jove is represented with three-forked lightning, Neptune with a trident, and Pluto with a three-headed dog. The Fates are three, the Furies three, the Graces three, the Harpies three, the Sibylline books three; and the Muses were three times three; the Pythoness sat on a tripod. Trinity is an aspect of divinity in all religions, and the Spiritual Law of Three is one of the most ancient spiritual laws.

Man is three-fold (body, soul, and spirit); the world is three-fold (earth, sea, and air); the enemies of man are three-fold (the world, the flesh, and the devil); the Christian graces are threefold (Faith, Hope, and Charity); the kingdoms of Nature are threefold (mineral, vegetable, and animal); the cardinal colours are three in number (red, yellow, and blue); we live in three dimensions.

The concept of the Three is very simple. Man and woman are needed to combine in order to create a child. The Law of Three is: "From one unto the second, whereupon the third must appear".

The Pythagoreans looked at the world in terms of harmony, and Three is the first point of harmony. One is Unity, godhead. Two is Duality, man and woman, etc. Three is manifestation, the first point of Stability. There is little doubt that, for the Pythagorean, the clearly defined 84 groups of three that are possible in the numbers One to Nine are important points of both mathematics and spirituality.

These are the Pythagorean Lines and Trines. Trinity is an ancient concept, and these 84 possible groups of Three in the Matrix are core to Pythagorean Numerology. As a note: The Divinity Dice Series by this author has a book dedicated to the Pythagorean Trines.

General Knowledge

There is no easy or direct proof to be found in historic texts regarding the Pythagorean Trines. In 1993 all the 84 patterns were found inscribed in the walls of a Temple to Pythagoras that had recently been unearthed. (76 Trines plus the 8 Lines make 84 possible combinations of Three in the Matrix) The Vedas state the universe exists for 84 Lacs (extended periods of time)

I took all this as an historical confirmation. I had been working with the Trines for over a decade with remarkable success, but to be clear, there is no written direct evidence supporting the claims of an authentic Pythagorean Tradition in this regard.

It is one of those things you initially take on faith, and as you gain experience you will realize how accurate they are.

One thing is certain, the Spiritual Law of Three was known and practiced in Pythagorean times. It is both reasonable and logical to assume that any set of three numbers that formed a relationship had direct meaning to the Pythagoreans.

Regardless of historical proof, common sense tells us that the 84 possible permutations of Three numbers in Nine were relevant to people who practiced the importance of Number in all things.

HOMEWORK:

Work out the Stated and Vacant TRINES in the Following Dates:

21 / 03 / 1987

29 / 11 / 1955

14 / 6 / 1932

(Take care to cover every possibility. There are lots of Trines here!)

When you are ready, move onto the next stage of study, which is:

Patterns in the Matrix

Patterns in the Matrix

By now we all have some idea of how to find an Aspect in the Matrix. We have gone over Noumenal Weight, Vacant Numbers, and how these create the Lines and Trines we use in interpretations. The next step is how all these can combine.

This next area of Pythagorean Numerology is little known and has been buried for centuries. It is important, and yet fairly simple. We take what we have learned about Aspects, and how to find them, then we combine all of these into PATTERNS. It is straightforward, and very easy to grasp once you are clear with the prior basics of how to find Trines and Lines in the Matrix.

There are 58 Patterns in all, with a small range of variations from the core Aspects.

Patterns become highly relevant when we do what we call OVERLAY Charts. We have shown a hint of these already, and following this chapter we will focus on the Overlay Matrix.

First we must learn how to discover if a PATTERN exists in any given Matrix, and then we can look at the concept of the Overlay (where Patterns occur quite frequently).

A Pattern is a collection of any active Lines or Trines in the Matrix. Any Active Line of Force, Line of Balance and Vacant Line or Set of Trines can combine to form a PATTERN.

Specific Patterns carry specific meanings, and they are used to cast a "landscape" picture of the general direction of the chart.

All that is required in this chapter is to learn to recognize when, and where, a Pattern is evident. This part is relatively simple.

The different types of Patterns are listed on the following pages with a graphic to give you a clear and definite overview of what each Pattern comprises. Once this is sorted, the Interpretations for these can be found in the Book of Interpretations.

Classifications of PATTERNS:

Patterns are grouped according to their "type". Each Pattern has a specific meaning, and when working with Overlay Matrix Charts, you will often find a number of Patterns presenting themselves. There are 58 basic Patterns. There are ancillary Patterns which we do not cover here, and which are for advanced study.

As always, the reader must decide what aspects have priority, and which are of less importance. As a note, certain aspects in a Matrix become stronger when the PRESENT DATE shares that aspect, or in particular when they meet and have close relations with a person who shares that aspect.

Once more, we describe each aspect with a clear graphic. If any given Matrix has a Line of Force, Vacant Line, or Line of Balance these can combine to create a Pattern.

Of note: INCOMPLETE Lines are far less likely to generate the influence of a Pattern, but it can happen in certain circumstances.

You will note most of the Patterns are described as a Letter from the Alphabet, and this is related in some distant manner to the nature of that letter, but really it is simply describing the SHAPE of the pattern. i.e. A "V" Pattern is in the shape of a "V".

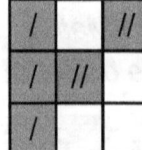 1-2-3 / 1-5-9 "V" Pattern here is demonstrated with the SHADED BOXES to describe the Pattern. In the graphics we will not include the "strokes" that indicate WHY is it a pattern, as we have in our example graphic here.

In the sample above you can clearly see the 1-5-9 Line of Force and the 1-2-3 Line of Balance. It's just this simple, two Lines combine to form a Pattern. The idea for now is all about learning to pick the Aspects that work together to form a Pattern.

As you get used to this process, finding the Patterns become self-evident. Again, learn to spot the Pattern, then go to the Book of Interpretations to sort out what importance they carry in the Matrix.

Book of Number: Practical

V Pattern

There are Eight possible combinations of "V" patterns in the Matrix, which are as follows:

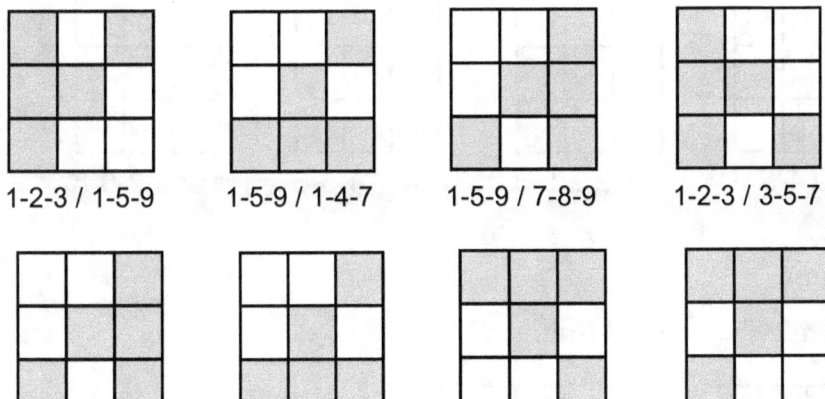

U Pattern

There are Four possible "U" Patterns, as follows:

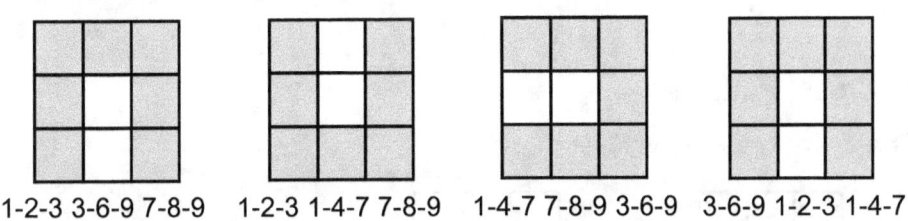

L Pattern

There are FOUR "L" Patterns. They are as follows:

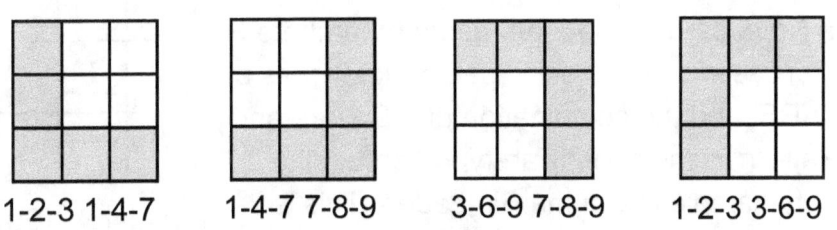

Book of Number: Practical

T Pattern

There are Four "T" Patterns, as follows:

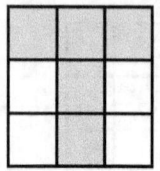 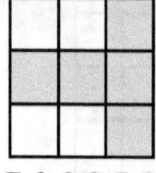 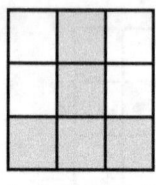 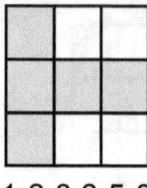

3-6-9 4-5-6   7-8-9 2-5-8   1-4-7 4-5-6   1-2-3 2-5-8

H Patterns

There are only Two "H" Patterns

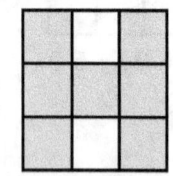 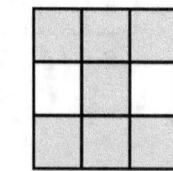

1-2-3 2-5-8 7-8-9   3-6-9 4-5-6 1-4-7

X (Cross) Patterns

There are only Two "X" Patterns

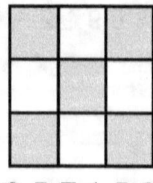 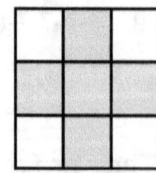

3-5-7 1-5-9   2-5-8 4-5-6

As a Note, can you see the "vacant" numbers here? These form a specific pattern known as a SQUARE, and the combination of a Square and "X" Pattern forms a messiah-type personality. A perfect example is Osama Bin Laden. This is an extremely potent combination where a sense of destiny overrides all else.

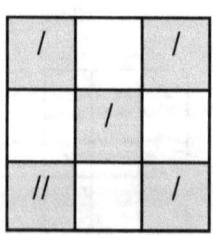

10 March 1957
Osama Bin Laden

Book of Number: Practical

Y Pattern

"Y" Patterns are effectively a "X" Pattern with a missing numeral. There are Eight in all, as follows:

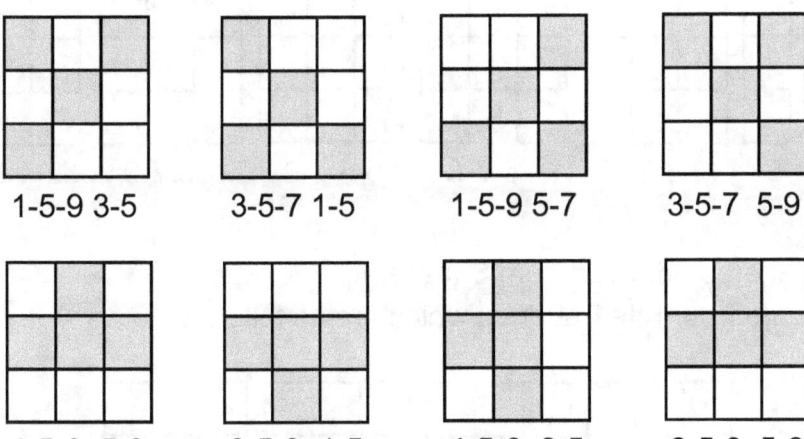

Z Patterns

There are Four "Z" Patterns, which are as follows:

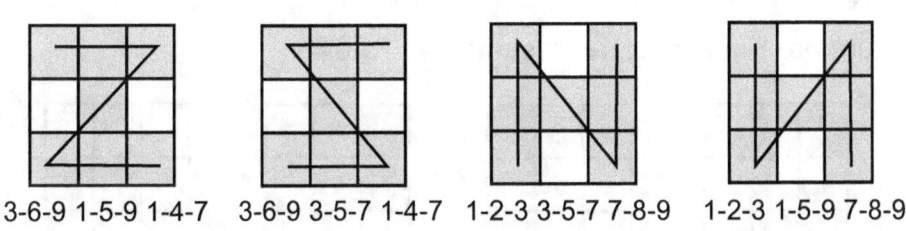

Epsilon Patterns

There are Four Epsilon Patterns, which are as follows:

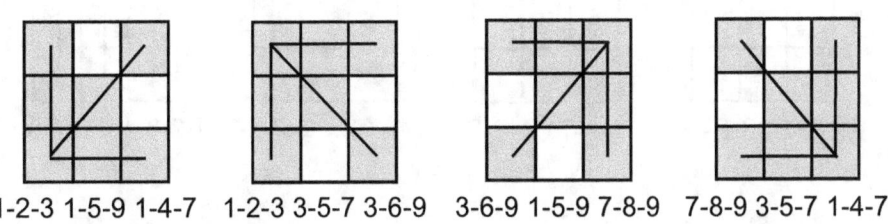

Square Patterns

There are Six possibilities, as follows:

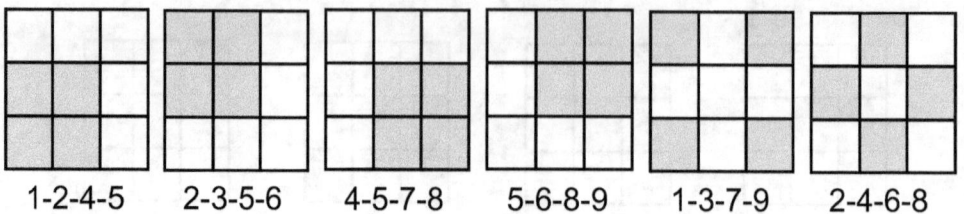

1-2-4-5   2-3-5-6   4-5-7-8   5-6-8-9   1-3-7-9   2-4-6-8

Kite Patterns (derived from Squares)

There are Four Kite Patterns, which are as follows:

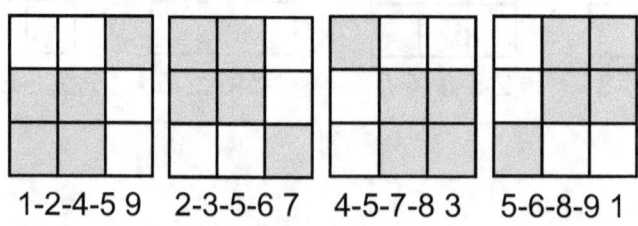

1-2-4-5 9   2-3-5-6 7   4-5-7-8 3   5-6-8-9 1

Parallel Patterns

There are Eight in all, represented as follows:

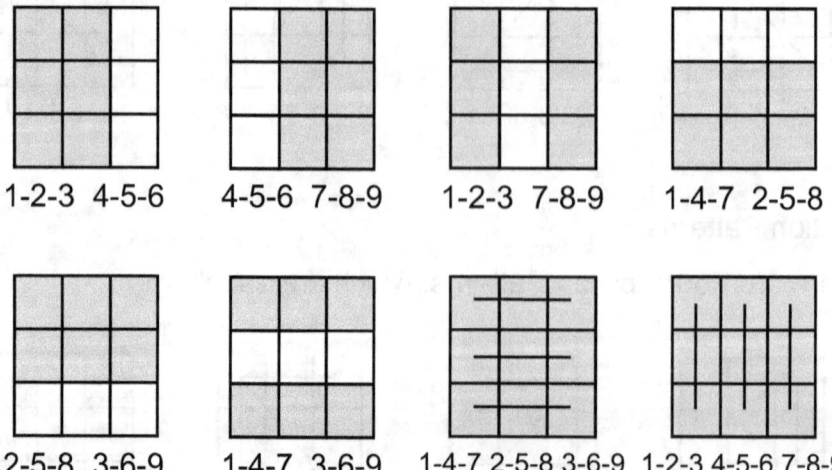

1-2-3 4-5-6   4-5-6 7-8-9   1-2-3 7-8-9   1-4-7 2-5-8

2-5-8 3-6-9   1-4-7 3-6-9   1-4-7 2-5-8 3-6-9   1-2-3 4-5-6 7-8-9

Book of Number: Practical

That is the sum total of Patterns in the Matrix. There are a number of variations where the weight of some number combines to make what seems a new Pattern.

12 3 1957

123 / 159

123 / 157

159 / 357

Three clear patterns occur on 12 3 1957. There are 2 x "V" Patterns (1-2-3 1-5-9 and 1-2-3 3-5-7) and the 1-5-9 3-5-7 Cross. These derive from the 1-2-3 Line of Force, 1-5-9 Line of Force and 3-5-7 Line of Balance.

You will note the Vacant 4-6-8 Trine is there as well? This stays as a strong aspect, whereas the Stated Trines are effectively "eaten up" by the Patterns.

2 3 1957

Small shifts can make a big difference. Change the date to 2 March 1957 and everything is different. You can see the major shift is a 1-3-7-9 Square active in this Chart, as well as the 1-5-9 3-5-7 Cross. A little shift in Number Weight can change everything.

But you can see that the 1-2-3 Line of Balance is not taken over by any Pattern? The 4-6-8 Vacant Trine is also prevalent. But what does this mean?

Reading a chart really requires understanding variables. Everything you do in working out Aspects really comes down to a balancing act. What is the stronger effect? If this person is married to someone born on that date, this introduces some other element that needs consideration. Variables are everywhere.

It is always a matter of judgement and perspective. No one can teach you perspective, only experience and feedback from clients will give you this. Here we learn the basics, which is how to find the Patterns themselves. Mark them out on a Matrix, make them a point of contact that people can physically see. As always, practice on whoever you can, and listen to what they have to say.

Book of Number: Practical

Remember: Everything in Numerology is a balancing act. This means that YOU have to be balanced. Take time, contemplate and come to centre every day. It is essential to opening up the inner divine channels to truth and wisdom.

Everything in giving a reading is dependent on how well you are a vehicle for the divine, and this means you must do several things.

A: You must love your work

B: You must never judge a Client

C: You must tell the truth as best you can

If you do not love what you do, all I can say is that the sacred channel that opens your heart to divine truth will stay shut.

Discrimination is one thing, but when you cross a line and judge a client, no matter how much you love your work, you will shut the door to spiritual inspiration.

If you fail to tell the truth as best you understand it, the energy that flows through you in a reading will become a ghost that haunts you.

In all, the advice is simple: *Do not tempt the Furies.*

HOMEWORK:

Determine the PATTERNS for the Following Dates

(No interpretations are necessary, you simply need to check if you have grasped the idea of how to find a Pattern)

21 May 1946

3 August 1976

19 August 1952

2 April 1956

Remember to practice on friends and relatives!

The Overlay Matrix

We now start to work with combining everything we have discussed to date into a cohesive, embracing dialogue. The Overlay Matrix is core to this, and is another Trinity: One chart, over another, creates a third.

Patterns in the Matrix are able to give a general direction to a person's chart at a glance. The OVERLAY PATTERNS are what allow you to quickly and easily see the major drives and energies at work between people, in employment, and in many other situations.

The questions a Numerologist will be asked are many and varied, but in essence most people want to know about three things.

A: Themselves
B: Their Relationships
C: Their Finances / Career

Overlay Charts can show you in moments if the person has natural affinity with a potential partner. Have they started a business on a fortuitous day? Is their current address harmonically suited to their present day goals? Basic life questions are solved.

It's quick, simple and easy.

The Overlay Charts are possibly the most powerful single tool in the Numerology toolbox, and in truth, it combines every tool you have into one, clear, authoritative form.

Once you have the basic understanding of how to read the various patterns and aspects in a Matrix Chart, the Overlay Matrix is the technique that extends your understanding of how a person fits in with those around them, and how the various aspects and potentials within themselves are best worked with.

The Overlay Matrix forms the last major hurdle we have to jump in the practical course. It is advised at this point to take up a study of Book III: Client Psychology, if you have not already done so.

The Overlay Matrix

We all know the old saying "No man is an island". All we need to do is connect with life and we can break the sense of isolation most suffer. But very few really achieve this. Most wander asking a simple question: Where is my rightful place, my home, in this sea of consciousness?

The Overlay Matrix quickly and easily shows the Querent where he stands in relation to others in his life (family and friends) and where he stands in relation to himself and present circumstances. The Overlay Matrix demonstrates in minutes the walls and bridges that are aspected in the individual's interactions with life.

The overlay technique is simply where we lay one Matrix over another, and see what evolves from this. As a common practice, we will overlay the Birth Matrix of a client over their Name Matrix to form a Combined Matrix. We also overlay the Birth Matrix of a client over the Birth Matrix of those in their immediate environment.

We consider the NAME Matrix as signifying the lineage a person carries. The Surname, or parental energy, modifies the natural birth energy. We look at both the Birth and Name Matrix individually. We find what Aspects are there, and then we OVERLAY the two to see what (if any) different Lines, Trines and Patterns emerge.

In simple terms, the OVERLAY provides the core energies that are awakened in the combination of any two given Matrix Charts.

Will you get on with a person you just met? Take the Matrix from your date of birth and place it over the Birth Matrix over the person in question. Is this a good day to start a business? Take your Date of Birth, and place it over the present day, and see what comes.

You will be amazed at how accurately it will describe the points of harmony and the areas of likely conflict between two individuals. The Overlay is extremely powerful in understanding relationships, likely business opportunities, and hidden pitfalls.

Book of Number: Practical

How does it work? Let's say Susan Mary Fox is thinking of marriage. She is born on 12 December 1978, and her potential husband is born on 1 June 1969. We map out the two Matrix Charts, and then OVERLAY them to see how compatible they may be.

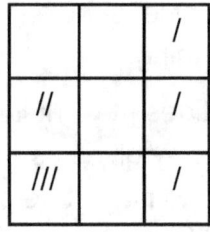
12 12 1978 MARY

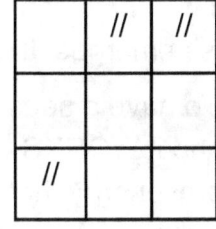
1 6 1969 BOB

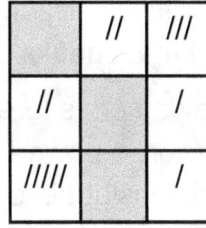
Overlay Chart

We have a few difficult Aspects at work in Mary's Birth Chart.

- Incomplete 1-2-3 Line of Force
- Vacant 4-5-6 Line + 7-8-9 Line of Balance
- 4-5-6 / 7-8-9 / 1-2-3 Triple Parallel (potential)

The man she is looking to marry is called Bob. He has a clear 1-6-9 Trine with every other Aspect affected by Vacant Number positions. Two Incomplete Lines of Balance, (1-5-9 and 3-6-9) Vacant Lines, (3-5-7 and 2-5-8) many Vacant Trines, a 1-6 Opposition, and also the difficult 5-6-7-8 Square and 5-6-7-8 / 3 Kite Patterns.

Both of these Birth Matrix Charts are very complicated, yet when we look at the OVERLAY MATRIX, all the complication vanishes. One SHARED Vacant 3-4-5 Trine is all that stands out. The complex Triple Parallel, and the difficult Square/Kite Patterns just vanish. You can IMMEDIATELY see the combination could just work.

So you look up the Aspect that is made. The Vacant 3-4-5 Trine is "A Fountain Waiting to Burst Forth". It seems to indicate the two may well be a good combination. Obstacles are removed, and life has the possibility of moving forward in a very positive manner. In minutes we have come to a possible positive for the two.

Book of Number: Practical

Now, I have not sat down and worked out every aspect, cataloged them, written them up, discussed the variable and potentials with the client, or done anything other than get a quick overview.

I can see in minutes that this is a workable match. Without knowing anything, common sense tells you that when a batch of complex and difficult Aspects vanish with an Overlay, and a nice, simple chart that speaks of progress emerges, it's a good thing.

Forewarned is forearmed. To have a sense of the tides at work in a situation is powerful stuff. And it WORKS. The Overlay gives us an instant insight into the general energy that comes into play. It helps us make better decisions and thus create a better life.

But let's go another logical step. We use the concept of the Overlay Matrix to set up a COMPARISON Matrix. There is another obvious layer to consider. Mary might take the man's last name when she marries, so what will THIS do in the context of her chart?

A prospective wife can work out the chart she will have when she changes her name to her husband's, and we can now COMPARE this against her old name. This will show in clear detail the areas where the marriage will be harmonious, and where it needs work.

Let's look at this. Susan Mary FOX is getting married and her name will change to Susan Mary HATHAWAY. It is now very easy to see what aspects are brought to focus:

Susan Mary

13115 4197

/	///	/
	/	
////	/	/

FOX

666

/		/
/	//	//
///////	/	//

HATHAWAY

81281517

120

Book of Number: Practical

You will note that the weight on the ONE is strong in all Matrix Charts: Birth, Overlay and Name. But with Hathaway the ONE is extremely pronounced. The Six vanishes. F = 6, O = 6, X = 6.

One Trine repeats (3-4-9) and one Trine (5-7-8) is created. The 1-5-8 and 1-4-7 Lines of Force remain, but do you notice how the 3-5-7 Line of Balance goes away? Fox has a: 1-5-9 / 3-5-7 "Cross" and a 1-5-9 / 1-4-7 "V" Pattern. The Cross disappears when she takes on the new Marriage Name. Remember, what is REMOVED can be as important as something new being brought into play.

Get the idea? It's all a moveable feast. The name change brings in a shifting tide of new circumstances. By going through the meaning for each of these changes we can describe the energetic direction that is likely to come out of the marriage.

After looking at these charts, I can say with absolute certainty that a marriage with Bob has excellent potential. I can't say if things will work out overall, because it's a marriage and it depends on two people continuing to like each other. But all things being equal, the charts look very positive for a life partner.

Get the idea? I didn't pull out all the Aspects, read them through, and get involved in hours of work. This only takes 2 minutes. With a quick overview we can accurately advise the client about the basic principles at work. Does she now wish to go into greater detail?

If the client does, we can start to look at the fine points, the likely points of agreement, compromise, and disagreement, etc. The whole point of the OVERLAY is to get an instant snapshot of the situation, and for this purpose it is remarkably accurate.

For many it is simply unbelievable that someone can summarize in under 2 minutes a situation they have been contemplating for months. But with the Overlay Matrix, this is just how it is.

This is the power of the Overlay. As you gain experience you start to accept that the Wisdom of the Ancients is at work, and that all you need do is grasp the reins and ride the horse.

Book of Number: Practical

But there are many more questions a client may need answered, and there is a basic Overlay you use with all clients. Specifically we look at the Name and Birth Combination. As you look at the example of Susan Fox below, pay attention to the Combined Matrix.

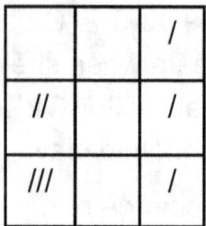
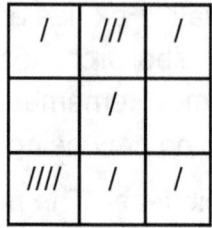

12 / 12 / 1978   Susan Mary FOX   COMBINED

Here we create an OVERLAY Matrix from the Birth Matrix and the Name Matrix. This gives us a fuller picture of the Patterns and Aspects at work within a client's life at a very basic level.

Without repeating all the Aspects we have already described in the birth date and the name, we can easily see in the OVERLAY chart the Dominant ONE, the 2-7-9 Trine, and the 4-5-8 Trine. A reading of these Aspects can be followed up with clarifying questions.

In essence, the 2-7-9 Trine determines that material issues are not a great concern. The core reason this person came here to Earth was to learn ACCEPTANCE. So we might ask, "Do you have any difficulty with acceptance of self, or others?"

The 4-5-8 Trine asks the question: Are we a Soul with a Body, or a Body with a Soul? So the combination of these two Aspects in this Overlay suggests we ask the Client the following:

- Do you feel you accept yourself as you are?
- Would you say your life has a Spiritual or Material focus?

What we are doing is not offering answers so much as planting seeds. We know these two points WILL be core issues at work in Susan Fox's life, but asking a question opens up more doors than statements of fact. When the heart opens, answers come naturally.

Book of Number: Practical

Let's focus on creating the Overlay. Below is a hypothetical example. Let's see if we can get the overview on how all this works.

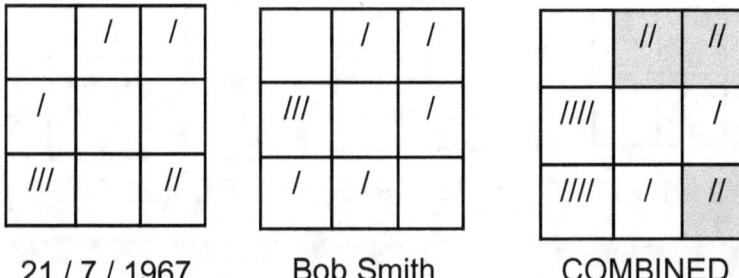

21 / 7 / 1967   Bob Smith   COMBINED

In the above example, a 6-7-9 Trine is brought into play with the Overlay Matrix. The basic guidance for this aspect is "At odds with your mind? Look into your heart." We can go through this with the client, to see how it fits in their life, but go further and look through the Matrix Patterns of siblings, marriage partners, parents and children to see where this pattern occurs in those charts.

You will be amazed at how often core Patterns, Lines and Trines repeat in the charts of Family Members.

These shared Aspects tell us the connections within the family unit. These can unravel a lot of the clues that a person needs to understand if they are to solve their personal puzzle box.

I simply cannot tell you the number of times a core Trine or Aspect has repeated in all but one member of a family, and I ask, "Is this person the Black Sheep?" So often you see a jaw drop, and the person says, "How could you have possibly known that?"

In Pythagorean Numerology, there is ONE CONSTANT. That is that there are NO COINCIDENCES. If a Trine or Pattern repeats, it means this is a karmic theme running through the family. The Overlay Matrix will so often reveal a pattern that is a constant to the entire family, and when it does, we know with absolute certainty that this will be describing a core issue for the individual.

We can also combine the Birth Date of the child with that of the parent, and see how they interact in the Overlay Matrix. (over)

Book of Number: Practical

21 / 7 / 1967   **13 / 10 / 1936**   **COMBINED**

In this Overlay Matrix, we see a Line of Balance across the Mind (3-6-9) Line, a series of Trines with 3-6-7 / 3-7-9 / 6-7-9 and most importantly a REPEATED VACANT TRINE that is common to both Birth Matrix Charts: the Vacant 4-5-8 Trine. The 4-5-8 Trine is a "Connecting Point" between parent and child. It is a Karma, or fixed point to be dealt with.

And obviously there are a number of other aspects as well.

We look up the interpretations of these Lines and Trines, and see how they fit into the overall picture. We are looking at the relationship between this client and their parent. It is truly extraordinary how things open up for people, particularly when they start getting insights into why they ended up with a particular parent.

And just as important as the above, we look at what DISAPPEARS when we overlay a Matrix. For the parent born 13 Oct 1936 the difficult 4-5-7-8 SQUARE PATTERN goes away, and the rebellious 3-4-8 Trine in the child leaves.

This tells me that a very serious or possibly even severe parent was raising a rebellious child, but when they both find agreement, humor and laughter is found, (Severe Square is broken in parent - rebellious nature is settled within the child) and the whole process leads to a refining of the mind. (3-6-9 Line of Balance)

There's much more to evolve from these Overlay Patterns in this situation, but are you grasping the basic principle? A Number Chart cannot stand alone. It is with the INTERACTIONS of those near and dear to us that the natural path of the person is made clear.

Book of Number: Practical

It is almost weird when you get the knack of all of this. You start with such basic details as a few dates of birth, and then you start telling people you have never met all about themselves.

I have had cynics put me to the test. They usually end up shouting at me saying, "This can't be true! Someone filled you in. No one can know that much about someone from just a few numbers!" And truth to tell, I don't. I am just reading from their Book of Number.

But I do enjoy those moments, and the look of shock on their face.

Remember these two things:

- There are no coincidences.
- Everything in our present life comes from the seeds sown (by ourselves or others) in the past.

I have found from long experience that the vast majority of people really don't have that many things they need to sort out. What they DO have is a whole lot of incomplete pieces, and no overall picture of where these need to go in order to make sense of things.

What you have before you with any client is a given set of circumstances that are like random pieces of a jigsaw. In understanding the "puzzle in pieces", you are really assembling a mirror for the person to look into, and get a picture of their reality. Once we know where the pieces fit, it is much easier to re-construct the jigsaw.

The Overlay Matrix is a simple, effective tool for demonstrating to a client a cross reference of a whole variety of influences that are likely to occur in their life. It is a tool that shows you how you are interacting with other people and situations. It is a mirror you can hold up to show the overall picture of a person's life

Your Birth Chart is an indicator of where you are at, but the Overlay Charts show you how, and where, your natural energy fits in with others. It is one of the most useful tools in the entire array of techniques available to you in Numerology.

On this point, you will note that I never do an Overlay Matrix with more than ONE person or situation at a time? This is important. We rarely do an Overlay with more than two birth dates, or two names, at any one time. The Spiritual Law of Three is at work here: *From the unity of the First and the Second, we produce the Third.*

For the present, keep all Overlay Charts to two events. These two create the third in the Overlay Chart. There are exceptions, but we want to avoid too much complexity at this point. Let's look at some appropriate applications.

Someone wants a new job? You can construct a Matrix from this person and the date of birth of the most relevant interaction they will have in the new company, usually the boss. If it is a large corporation, use the founding date for the company and the birth date of the client

Someone is thinking of traveling to a new city? Obviously, when the city was founded is it's date of birth, so we use this as the second Matrix. Getting the idea? We use a birth date with a founding date, NOT a birth date with the name of the city. Like meets like.

The Overlay describes WHAT WILL MANIFEST between the interaction of any two realities. It is a very quick, yet powerful tool.

HOMEWORK:

Take anyone you know, and practice using Overlay Matrix patterns. This time, practice creating an Overlay Matrix using their parents and loved ones. Get some feedback, and prove it for yourself!

From an Earlier Homework, take the following names and date, and OVERLAY the Name Matrix with the Birth Matrix.

John Jones
30 June 1956

Patricia Hamilton
14 May 1939

Gregory Dalton
12 Jan 1927

Doublets and Magic Squares

We have now covered the basic techniques for finding Aspects in a persons name and date of birth. There are many small refinements to all we have covered so far, and many areas (such as Cycles) that warrant an entire book to themselves.

However, the goal is to get you moving with Numerology, not to have you stuck in 7 years of study.

Doublets, however, are very common and in some cases are also important to understanding a chart. While it appears they break the "Rule of Three" that so much of Pythagorean Numerology is wrapped around, they don't. The two elements create the third.

We think of doublets as a sort of question that is being asked. The answer to what they ask creates the third element, or Trine.

We also take a look at the Magic Square Chart, and offer a way to work this into your interpretations. This simple map of numbers is a mathematical perfection, and from here ratio and many other ancient equations were evolved.

Do not be concerned if you find the Magic Squares a little difficult to grasp. It is one of the refinements that can take years to get your head around.

DOUBLETS: (Oppositions)

Doublets, or Oppositions, occur in many charts. They are not a highly significant influence EXCEPT when there are THREE Doublets in the Matrix.

This is extremely unlikely to occur in a Birth Date, but it is possible. If it does, the Triple Doublet tends to become a ruling force in that persons life, and it also tends to be a difficult obstacle to climb over. The Doublet is often called an "opposition" because it sets up opposing forces in a person's life, and it is not an easy aspect to deal with. That is the nature of Oppositions, but in climbing over them we become much stronger.

The definition of a Doublet is simply ANY TWO NUMBERS that are equally represented, where there is no third number sharing the same weight.

///		//
	/	//
/		///

Hypothetical Matrix

Triple Doublets are very unlikely to occur in a birth date, but can occur in names

In this example we see the 1-5 / 3-7 / 8-9 all sharing equal weight as pairs, and there are three such pairs. This describes a relationship of tension between the three specific pairs. One/Five is identified with the Feminine Ego, Three/Seven relates a conflict between the spiritual and the material, and the Eight/Nine represents issues connected with control and being in charge.

In a nutshell, the interpretation is that the individual needs to find and listen to the Inner Voice, and allow higher powers to provide them guidance. What we have opposing this is the conflict between our sense of self-worth (how we are seen), our need for security (how we survive) and a need to know our purpose in life (our direction) and obviously, how we can resolve all these tensions.

This is esoteric Numerology, and to really understand these subtle aspects you need an extraordinarily clear grasp on what each number represents and how it interacts with the other numbers.

Book of Number: Practical

Suffice to say, when you see these aspects, it is like the person is being stopped internally, and asked a question. It is very hard for people with these oppositions in their chart to feel "free flowing", yet so often you will find people who NEED to be spontaneous (actors, comedians, etc.) will have some sort of opposition at work.

There are 36 oppositions possible in a Matrix:

1-2	2-3	3-4	4-5	5-6	6-7	7-8	8-9
1-3	2-4	3-5	4-6	5-7	6-8	7-9	
1-4	2-5	3-6	4-7	5-8	6-9		
1-5	2-6	3-7	4-8	5-9			
1-6	2-7	3-8	4-9				
1-7	2-8	3-9					
1-8	2-9						
1-9							

Shaded areas indicate natural oppositions

In many ways, these oppositions are interpreted by the mind as a question. The 1 - 2 Opposition is like the inner mind is asking "Where can I find balance". That part is simple. What it does not interpret is what Balance is for the individual. For a Nazi, seeing a swastika might be a thing of exceedingly good fortune, yet for a Jew, it is hardly likely to represent that same thing. So, if you are the reader of a chart where a 1 - 2 opposition is to be found, you need to find out what symbolizes balance to that person.

ALL Doublets / Oppositions are inherently unstable aspects. They pose unanswered questions and indicate a deep yearning or seeking force within the person they inhabit.

Here it is important to touch on a deep understanding, that anything we see represented in a Number Chart is really an ECHO of what is resonating inside the person. These Aspects are like "Spiritual Magnets". Depending on how a person is polarized, they are attracting or repelling the energies inherent in their natal chart.

MAGIC SQUARES

There is also a very deep aspect of the Opposition where we chart the person's matrix with their BIRTH Number at the center of the Matrix, and use the appropriate "Magic Square" that has this number at it's pivot.

8	1	6
3	5	7
4	9	2

Magic Square

3	6	9
2	5	8
1	4	7

Matrix

If someone is a FIVE by birth, we use the traditional Magic Square with the 5 in the center. They have a 1 - 2 opposition, and we "transpose" the position of the 1 - 2 over the normal Matrix and we find the "answer" is with the 6 - 7

This is getting to the extremely complicated subtle points, but if someone is asking "Where is my Balance" the answer is in the area of the 6 - 7 Opposition "Where is my Certainty?"

So, short answer, the area of balance for the person comes from a feeling of certainty. I mention this, because if you ask a person with a 1 - 2 opposition where they believe their balance is, they will have no idea. That's what the problem is. However, if you ask them "Is there any area in your life you feel a sense of certainty?" you will hear them say things like, "I felt really right on Grandma's knee when she told me stories."

8	1	6	8	1	6	8	1	6
3	5	7	3	5	7	3	5	7
4	9	2	4	9	2	4	9	2
8	1	6	8	1	6	8	1	6
3	5	7	3	5	7	3	5	7
4	9	2	4	9	2	4	9	2
8	1	6	8	1	6	8	1	6
3	5	7	3	5	7	3	5	7
4	9	2	4	9	2	4	9	2

Here is the full magic square chart. If someone is a Six birth number, go to the Six in this chart and use the numbers surrounding it to find the Magic Square that relates to the Six.

Note that only the square with the Five in the centre gives the addition of 15 on all of the various axis.

As you explore the FEELING of this for the individual, the answer of what is balance (or whatever the opposition might be) for them will often arise.

Doublets / Oppositions always indicate a challenge for the Querent. They are never an easy ride, and rarely harmonious. But this is not "bad", and the truth is, if the person works through these energies, they come out of the troubles significantly better equipped for life.

Remember: If gravity were to increase by 20% tomorrow, everyone would be 20% stronger within a few weeks. That is the reality of opposition, it makes us stronger.

Natural Oppositions in the Matrix:

It is worth noting that in this series there are 8 sets of Doublets that ALWAYS indicate tension. These are the ones that go from a corner and "cross over" the natural lines or axis in a chart.

These specific Aspects always speak of internal conflict and tension in the mind or heart of the Querent. As always, Doublets pose a question, but the natural oppositions are Aspects that relate to Core Karma, or deep issues that must be addressed if an individual is to make genuine progress in this life.

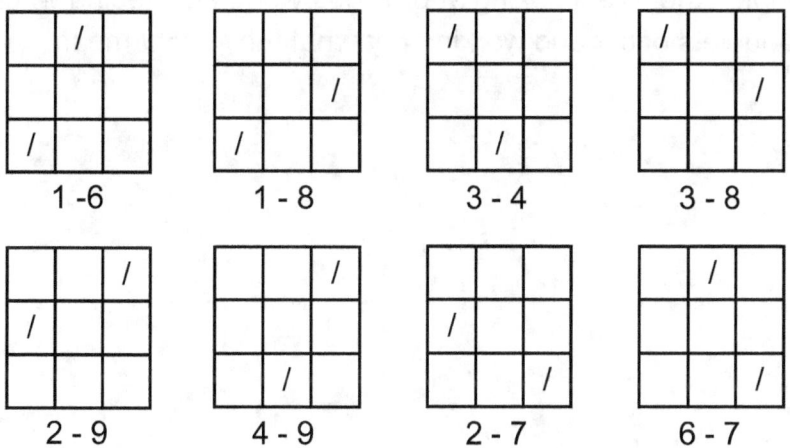

Once more, we are touching on Esoteric Numerology here, and this is really for advanced students. I include it more for you to keep in mind, because (in time) subtle points like these make a great deal of difference as to how you interpret a chart.

As you read Oppositions in a Chart, remember they are really unanswered questions. When the client discovers an internal answer to these Aspects, they change and become a sort of personal statement.

Oppositions are like a dam that slows you down until you learn to harness the energy, and letting the energy go in the right way means you generate power and gain a sense of authority. They can lead to the client developing a very strong sense of self-worth and confidence.

We give you a Doublet chart on the following pages and include the question each Doublet asks. In many ways, all you need do here is simply listen for what the answer might be for your client. You may well get a sense of someone whispering you an answer when you focus. This whole area is very open to possibility, and the reader has to trust their instincts regarding what direction to go here.

There is no specific Homework for this closing section of the practical book, other than looking at previous work, and seeing where the Doublets occur and working out what they might mean.

Book of Number: Practical

Interpretive Questions for DOUBLETS

1-2	2-3	3-4	4-5	5-6	6-7	7-8	8-9
1-3	2-4	3-5	4-6	5-7	6-8	7-9	
1-4	2-5	3-6	4-7	5-8	6-9		
1-5	2-6	3-7	4-8	5-9			
1-6	2-7	3-8	4-9				
1-7	2-8	3-9					
1-8	2-9						
1-9							

1-2 "Where is my Balance?"

1-3 "How do I fit in?"

1-4 "How do I find Certainty?"

1-5 "Who Am I?"

1-6 "Do I Trust?"

1-7 "Who or what will Complete me?"

1-8 "What is Wealth?"

1-9 "How do I Take Charge?"

2-3 "What is Acceptable?"

2-4 "How do I Profit?"

2-5 "What is the reason I am Here?"

2-6 "Why do I feel so Alone?"

2-7 "How do I Focus?"

2-8 "Why do I Feel so much?"

Book of Number: Practical

2-9 "Where is True Harmony?"

3-4 "What is Truth?"

3-5 "Why do we Sing?"

3-6 "How can I mend the Mind"

3-7 "Where is my Adventure"

3-8 "How do I set my Sail?"

3-9 "How do I Let Go?"

4-5 "Will I refuse Society?"

4-6 "Why do I feel Driven?"

4-7 "What do I need to Survive?"

4-8 "Where is my Soul?"

4-9 "How can I take Charge?"

5-6 "What is my True Nature?"

5-7 "Where does the River Flow?"

5-8 "Where is the Profit?"

5-9 "How do I Focus?"

6-7 "How does this Add Up?"

6-8 "Who and/or What do I Need?"

6-9 "Where are my Limits?"

7-8 "What do I Deserve?"

7-9 "How can I Serve?"

8-9 "How does a Flower Open?"

Newton's Three Laws of Motion

1. An object at rest will remain at rest unless acted on by an unbalanced force. An object in motion continues in motion with the same speed and in the same direction unless acted upon by an unbalanced force.

2. Acceleration is produced when a force acts on a mass. The greater the mass (of the object being accelerated) the greater the amount of force needed (to accelerate the object).

3. For every action there is an equal and opposite re-action.

A simple way of looking at Newton's Laws is to consider the 15th century writer and doctor, Paracelsus and his axiom on Trinity: *From the First unto the Second, whereupon the Third must appear.*

When you have two active properties, a third property will be produced. The same applies to Number. When you have two numbers in interaction, the chemistry between these two with produce an effect of some sort.

The difference between the Trine and the Doublet is that with the Trine, the third property is known. The energy of the Trine is like a pyramid with a triangle base. The three elements combine to create the forth, which is in effect creating a three dimensional form.

A Doublet creates a third energy, but it is not defined or made certain. This is why the energy created is posed as a question.

Symbology

There are many small details that round off the Practical Course and in this last chapter we will take a brief look at some of the small details that complete the core of being able to effectively read a Numerology Chart.

Generally, most charts are fairly obvious, but every one of them is a puzzle box. These last tools are helpful in fine-tuning the tools to pick apart the odd things that can and do crop up in a chart.

The MOST IMPORTANT tool is one I cannot describe in detail and where experience is the only teacher. This is the area Jung loved, the internal SYMBOLOGY of clients, and the experience of omens.

Symbols and Omens

We all know a Nazi sees a swastika and experiences a very different set of emotions than a Jew looking at the same symbol. This is simply to highlight the fact that all those cheap dime store books that state a symbol in a dream, etc. means a specific thing do not take into account the personal internal dialogue of the individual.

A Symbol is like a "date of birth" that interacts with us in the same way as we would view an overlay matrix. Its meaning is entirely dependent on the personal relationship an individual shares with it. The same goes for omens, dream images, etc.

Now there is no clear tool we can use to determine what a symbol means for a client other than Occam's Razor. This is essentially that the simplest explanation is often the most correct.

To make this simple, if I have a person dreaming of a swastika, the first question I would ask is "What is your heritage?". If they are Jewish, I have a line of thought to follow that is obvious. If they are Tibetan, there is a different line of thought. (The swastika was taken out of Tibet and used by the Nazis)

Rarely are the symbols, omens and portents a client experiences easy to determine, but when you do work out a core message, it is always something obvious, and extremely meaningful.

Symbols and omens are the language the inner being uses to communicate to the external consciousness. Jung saw symbols as a bridge between the conscious and unconscious self. One classic example is of a client who saw an "arm on the sun". This is what started him on his quest to grasp what it might mean.

At first Jung just thought it was a strange manifestation of the man's unconscious mind, but many years later, he read how the Zoroastrians had written thousands of years earlier of the same symbol. He realized the man experienced a Universal Symbol, and out of this he evolved his study of the "Cosmic Unconsciousness".

Rupert Shelldrake's theory of "Morphic Resonance" also ties in with our study of symbology. This is a principle where Life communicates to itself via "life resonance". Life communicates messages to all of life in a multitude of ways, but for we higher apes, life often talks to us in SYMBOLS.

When you have a certain energy set up in your being, and you are drawing or repelling similar or opposing energies, you set up a clarion call on the subtle levels. This "call" creates a doorway through which energy comes.

The "doorway" is experienced as a symbol or omen. The Tibetans refer to this as Mudra, or "opening". The Mudra is really everything that has gone into creating it: the opening, the bricks that built the doorway, as well as the process it takes the individual to get to this point. And at the core of it all is the KEYSTONE.

At the core of every symbol or omen a person experiences there is simple, obvious keystone. It is, as the word implies, the "key" to understanding the entire process.

Let's look at a few real life examples that came to me, and as we walk through the experience this may become more clear.

A man came to me once. He was puzzled, had no clear direction in life, and he had recently had a powerful experience where he felt a huge train was coming from behind, about to run him down.

You might think this is a little strange, but at the time the fellow was deep in contemplation, sitting in a chair. The experience was so strong he literally threw himself from the chair, in order to get out of the way of the train.

Now, he was living in a house beside a river. The place had no road or rail access, so we can safely assume there was no train. I asked carefully, and made sure there were no train tracks in the vicinity. Why? Because in contemplation we can get an amplification of senses, and a distant train can seem very close.

This is an ARCHETYPAL experience. We hear it in the Negro spirituals and in such classics as "Freight Train". The train comes to take you to freedom.

The client went into detail. It was a powerful experience, with the sound of a whistle, the rattle of the train on the tracks, and a sense of some impending power coming down and about to run through him.

In the archetypal experience, it is salvation, the coming of a high power to take you to a new and better world. In other words, what it really means is death, of a sort. The man jumps out of the way, so his survival instinct takes charge and he avoids death.

With further questioning, it turns out the man had been suffering extreme hardship, had barely been able to eat for 2 years because of health conditions, and by the size of him (he wore girl size 24 inch jeans in his early 20's) I imagined that was true. So I could interpret that symbol to mean that he had ducked the bullet. He had gotten past the health conditions and was on the road to recovery.

So what would have happened if he had not instinctively jumped to the side? The man thought he had missed a spiritual experience because of fear. I had to consider carefully before I responded. "Were you afraid of dying?" I asked.

He laughed. "No, just the pain of getting run down by a train."

"Have you suffered a lot of pain?"

The fellow broke down, and told me his life had been pain. Physical, emotional, and mental pain had been with him since puberty. Herein lies the keystone. His actions were saying he no longer wanted the pain, the pain that had been with him since puberty.

So from the archetypal message of the train, we interface the personal experience of the individual. The hard part is working out how the two mix. I could see the man was very dedicated to spiritual pursuits, possibly as a way to escape his personal pain.

Well, it doesn't take a lot to figure that he probably had issues around sex, but that is almost everyone. I needed more information. "What other experiences have you had that were powerful like this one?"

He then described an extraordinary spiritual experience where he felt he was part of the power of the universe. He had seen a column of light, and stepped into it. He felt the universe flowing through him, both ancient and new, enormous and minute. Every possibility was encompassed in that single moment he stepped into that column of light.

Here, I knew the archetype was that of the Messiah, the eternal savior consciousness. It is a real thing, and whether you believe it is Jesus, or Buddha, doesn't matter. The experience is that the present collapses, and the totality of all things flow through you.

The man had a spiritual destiny to fulfil. I had no idea what it might be, but it gave me a focal point. Now as I worked out his chart I could frame things with this in mind. He had chosen to live, and he had a destiny to fulfil.

I know this may sound incredibly simple. We like to think symbols mean great and important things, but the reality is that they are simple messages. They may not be specific. In fact, they are almost always cryptic, but the general direction is always obvious.

On another occasion I had a client who had decided to fall in love with me. When a person meets someone who seems to hold mysterious power, this is often the case. In this instance the woman had dreams which led her to believe we should be married.

Now, dream experiences of union with a teacher are very common, archetypal messages of a connection. But the sexual interpretation of this comes from personal needs. It is a common experience for doctors and practitioners with authority to have patients fall in love with them. It isn't necessarily right, but it is common.

The core reason why doctors are struck off if they have sexual relations with patients is specifically because these power/sex relationships are so well known, and so fraught with problems.

In this case, I took the woman out to a park, and asked her to close her eyes and tell me when she felt as I came closer. Now we all have an aura, a field of energy, about us. This interacts with others in differing ways, and when someone is in our proximity, the interaction between two auric fields is very distinct.

I asked her to think of the first thing that came to her mind, other than myself, when she felt my aura touch hers. I specifically told her it would NOT be something connected to myself, but some deeper dream she had held for years. Now this is cheating. As any NLP practitioner will tell you, I am programming her mind with a trigger to stimuli. But I am not telling her WHAT to trigger to.

She says "Bookstore! I always wanted to run a bookstore!"

So cutting to the chase, she has an archetypal attraction, but the core of it was that she had deep urges to complete her life. Her outer mind perceived this as having a man complete her, but her inner self want to take charge of life, and be self-employed.

Now, that is one part of the story. The other part is looking for the confirmation in the Chart. Here I admit that I already knew the woman's concern, because it was self-evident in her chart.

She had a 4-6-8 Vacant Trine in a pivotal position, which always indicates the need for self-employment. What was happening is a simple process, and we look at this in the Spiritual Psychology of Number. She was cross-pollinating natural desires. Her need for self-employment and her need for love got crossed when she met a successful, self-employed man.

When she realized she wanted to open a bookshop, her infatuation with me vanished. What's more, she opened the bookshop and this changed her entire life. She moved from needing to doing.

A former student of the course wanted to change her name. A new name had been given to her in a dream and she came to me and asked for a numerical assessment. The clear, unambiguous answer was "NO!" Everything about her new name was difficult.

This was a young lady who had gone through the correspondence course you now have in your hands as a book. She was one of the better students, and the first question I asked was, "You can do this yourself, why do you want to pay me?"

She explained she was too close to it, but the dream symbol was very strong, and she felt compelled to change her name, and wanted external verification. Well, she got the opposite, but changed her name anyway. Her life turned to ruin. She met, fell in love, and was then hunted for two years by a strange man who apparently had been attracted to her immediately after she changed her name.

So she came back and asked what she could do. I said "Change you name back to the boring one you didn't like. Failing that, move to another city." She moved to another city.

The point is, what she experienced was a FALSE vision. It was a mock-up generated internally from her desire to escape convention. This aspect was strongly noted in her chart. Herein lies another important thing to grasp about Symbols.

How do we determine a "mock-up" from a genuine omen? I know a women who stopped a former husband seeing his child because "God told her he should stay away", etc. How can we tell if it is BS or Blessing? We use commonsense and the number chart.

If you believe a symbol means a particular thing, but there is nothing in the chart to confirm it, you need to reassess things.

I have a wonderful friend who, when I met him, was looking for his spiritual path. He had a clear, defined message given to him. He would meet a spiritual teacher called BABA LARTON. He received this name in the dream state, but he had searched and found no guru or teacher called this. But it was a clear message, a great teacher called Baba Larton would direct him to his true path.

My friend came with me to a small convention run by a spiritual group. People were giving talks, but he wasn't all that interested, and we chatted in the background. Then an American man came on stage, and said in a soft New Jersey drawl, "My name is Bob Lawton". My friend jumps out of his seat.

"That's him! That is who I saw! What was his name?" He asks.

For some reason, the man said his name again, "Bob Lawton". In a soft New Jersey drawl this sounds exactly like "Baba Larton". My friend joined the group, and is still with them some 25 years later.

What I thought was an odd symbol was, in truth, a fact.

This is where the greatest asset in learning and understanding Number comes into play. We are building an internal and external language that life can now use to communicate with us. Life can speak to us DIRECTLY via Number. As soon as you ask a genuine question, life will present you with a numerical answer.

As a classic example, I had been considering converting the old Numerology correspondence course into book form for some time. One night, as I came back to consciousness, the number "51" was presented to me very clearly. This symbol meant it was time to start writing. How do we understand what a symbol means? Practice.

So if you think this is all too much work, blame Number 51!

Letters and their Meanings:

When you are looking at someone's name and you are trying to get a feel for them, you can tell a lot from little things like the letters in their name.

In understanding the meaning of letters as they apply to a person, look to the FIRST CONSONANT and the FIRST VOWEL in EACH of the NAMES given at BIRTH. e.g. PEter JAmes RObertson.

Let's look at the name Peter.

"P" Penetrating/Observant/Freedom Loving

"E" Intellectual/Clear/Communicative

All "Peters" share these qualities to a greater or lesser degree.

Note: If the first letter is a vowel, do not consider other letters in the name unless it is a DOUBLE VOWEL, as in AAron. This effectively doubles the energy of this vowel.

Why is this so? Your name is really your first interaction with the outside world. The use of language carries with it a certain power, and the repeated use of a tone or phrase embeds itself into the consciousness . The "Pe" sound in Peter is something that "Peter" has heard his entire life when someone spoke to him.

When language was formed, it was the great creative effort that turned us from being mere apes into human consciousness. Scientists look for the "missing Link" but in simple truth, language is the transforming shift in consciousness. The formation of thought into the structure of communication is core to all civilization. Language is wrapped around the "life tones", the vowel tones were integral to what the Greeks called the Ekstasis, or audible life stream .

You can hear these tones often as a high pitched sound in or around the ears. These are heard as core sounds, or vowel tones, and from here the consonants shape this energy into language.

The first two letters of the name have the greatest significance. The others have some effect, but overall this is more a part of the general Numerical Chart, and in particular the Matrix Chart.

Book of Number: Practical

A brief summary of the POSITIVE aspects of the letters are:

"A" Forthright, Direct, Considered

"B" Gentle, Determined, Curious

"C" Soft, Perceptive (Cecil) or Hard, Single Minded (Carol)

"D" Considerate, Demure, Effeminate

"E" Intellectual, Clear, Communicative

"F" Dreamlike, Fey, Expressive

"G" Warm, Coaxing, Kind

"H" Broad of Thought, Reaching, Home-Loving

"I" Sharp Focus, Clarity, Awareness

"J" Judgement, Strength, Contained

"K" Open, Discriminating (soft) or Determined (hard)

"L" Changeable, Flexible, Contemplative

"M" Persuasive, Expansive, Magnanimous

"N" Permanent, Stubborn, Fixed

"O" Open, Embracing, Containing

"P" Penetrating, Observant, Freedom Loving

"Q" Questioning, Negotiable, Businesslike

"R" Rich, Power Conscious, Strong

"S" Subtle, Transparent, Shifting

"T" Teacher, Tense, Tactful

"U" Understanding, Benevolent

"V" Vivacious, Violent, Vindictive

"W" Willful, Determined, Unbending

"X" Hidden, Silent, Stealthy

"Y" Thoughtful, Curious, Questioning

"Z" Honest, Direct, Unimpressed by Flummery

Determining Energetic Direction

Usually a vowel determines whether the character of "C" and "K" is hard or soft. The name Karin can be pronounced KAH-rin or KA-rin. The K-AH is a soft "K", while KA creates a hard "K".

All these positive aspects can become reversed. All aspects are simply an energy, and subject to duality. Obviously with people and also with any Aspect, there is a positive and a negative value.

And equally as obvious, it goes both ways. If there is a Negative Aspect in a personality it can REVERSE to a positive one, and vice versa. This is a basic principle that is true throughout ALL Number Science.

We are all fish swimming in an ocean of tides. So how do we determine the direction of the tide? How do we know we are moving in the right direction energetically?

Gosh! Do you think it might have something to do with having your Number Chart read by a professional?

In most cases we see a swinging between the positive and negative characteristics inherent within an individual. This is normal, and depending on the circumstances and attitude of the person/s concerned, the "swing" will be greater or lesser. It should be noted that even in the most apparently stable of individuals, this energy is still moving, from the Positive to the Negative poles of their personality.

The truly Neutral person is the one who has managed to master this aspect of their Being.

And so our overall goal is to assist a person to become NEUTRAL in their relationship with Society and external matters. When someone is neutral to external influences, their natural direction will flow as surely as a river flows to the sea.

HARMONIC BALANCE: (Higher Numerology)

Following on from the energy of letters in a name, each person carries a "harmonic signature". This can be resolved quite easily. The birth and name Matrix will show the key note a person is connected to, and the frequencies they have to work with in their life.

To be more specific, each person "modulates" along certain, specific "lines" of energy. You can HEAR this energy, often as a high-pitched ringing in or around your ears. It is the Voice of Life speaking to you. As you interact with this Sound Current, the latent patterns and aspects in your chart resonate and come to life.

This interaction forms what the Vedic teaching calls SHABDA or BANI. The Greeks called it Ekstasis, and in the Bible it is called "The Word". The range of Harmonic Energy is infinite in a sense, but it follows the mathematics of the 12 Tone Scale.

How can this be so? The 12 tone scale represents a HARMONIC FORM or MODEL that the universe appears to be in agreement with. Between any two notes in the 12 tone scale, we can evolve another 12 tone scale, and so on. Like a Hall of Mirrors, the sound current cycles within itself to an infinite degree.

There are four basic levels of this "tone current" that is in accordance with the Four Querent Types. The Ascending / Descending poles, and the Internalizing / Externalizing poles. See: The Four Querent Types (In Client Psychology)

On the technical side... Each Number is represented by a musical note. "A" = One, "A#" = Two, and so on up the musical scale to 12 = "Ab". The Universal Number Chart is as follows:

1	2	3	4	5	6	7	8	9	10	11	12
A	Bb	B	C	Db	D	Eb	E	F	Gb	G	Ab

Practical: Someone is born on the 12 August 1987
This equates to: 1+2+8+1+9+8+7 = 36. 3+6 = 9 = the Key of "F"

Book of Number: Practical

Obviously this is the start point. The Birth Number is a central point of focus in a chart, so to the Key Note. It is its interaction with the other points of reference in a chart that gives its true meaning.

If this area of study is something that fascinates you, there is a great deal more information at www.numberharmonics.com. This is the main thrust of study I worked with after I had completed this course on Numerology that you now hold.

The core of this study is that every relationship you can develop in Numerology has a mirror relationship you can describe harmonically. I can literally PLAY someone's birth chart on a musical instrument and I have many instances of truly remarkable responses from clients when I have done this

I was testing this out years ago and I had a young woman come up to me at a New Age fair where I had a booth. She was curious and asked for a tape to be recorded for her (Yes, before the days of CD's). I quickly assessed her chart and did a 15 minute recording.

Now I knew nothing about this person, and I didn't do an intense analysis on her chart other than to point out that there seemed to be a difficult aspect regarding her father. She seemed to think this was wrong, but I recorded that aspect even so. It was very clear to me that the Overlay Matrix showed a specific and difficult pattern when I ran her father's chart over the top of hers.

She listened while I recorded it, and went away with the tape.

Twenty minutes later she came back, very angry and unable to speak above a whisper. She demanded to know what I did. I was a little surprised at the ferocity of this seemingly peaceful girl, but I asked "Are you absolutely certain there was no issue with your father, specifically around the age of 12?"

The penny dropped. She went white, and her voice came back to her. "He was always telling me to be quiet and stop talking so much. Every day, that was all he said. I felt completely un-loved."

There is great power in the Harmonics of Number.

Book of Number: Practical

An Introductory Chart for Harmonic Numbers

(Please keep in mind, this is a very basic overview)

Birth Number: One
Musical Key: A
Most Inharmonious Numbers: 2 7
Most Harmonious Numbers: 1 3 5 6 8 10 12
Relative Minor Numbers: 4 9 11

Birth Number: Two
Musical Key: A# / Bb
Most Inharmonious Numbers: 3 8
Most Harmonious Numbers: 2 4 6 7 9 11 1
Relative Minor Numbers: 5 10 12

Birth Number: Three
Musical Key: B
Most Inharmonious Numbers: 4 9
Most Harmonious Numbers: 3 5 7 8 10 12 2
Relative Minor Numbers: 6 11 1

Birth Number: Four
Musical Key: C
Most Inharmonious Numbers: 5 10
Most Harmonious Numbers: 4 6 8 9 11 1 3
Relative Minor Numbers: 7 12 2

Birth Number: Five
Musical Key: C# / Db
Most Inharmonious Numbers: 6 11
Most Harmonious Numbers: 5 7 9 10 12 2 4
Relative Minor Numbers: 8 1 3

Birth Number: Six
Musical Key: D
Most Inharmonious Numbers: 7 12
Most Harmonious Numbers: 6 8 10 11 1 3 5
Relative Minor Numbers: 9 2 4

Book of Number: Practical

Birth Number: Seven
Musical Key: D# / Eb
Most Inharmonious Numbers: 8 1
Most Harmonious Numbers: 7 9 11 12 2 4 6
Relative Minor Numbers: 10 3 5

Birth Number: Eight
Musical Key: E
Most Inharmonious Numbers: 9 2
Most Harmonious Numbers: 8 10 12 1 3 5 7
Relative Minor Numbers: 11 4 6

Birth Number: Nine
Musical Key: F
Most Inharmonious Numbers: 10 3
Most Harmonious Numbers: 9 11 1 2 4 6 8
Relative Minor Numbers: 12 5 7

Birth Number: Ten
Musical Key: F# / Gb and Gbm / Eb
Most Inharmonious Numbers: 11 4
Most Harmonious Numbers: 10 12 2 3 5 7 9
Relative Minor Numbers: 1 6 8

Birth Number: Eleven
Musical Key: G and Gm / E
Most Inharmonious Numbers: 12 5
Most Harmonious Numbers: 11 1 3 4 6 8 10
Relative Minor Numbers: 2 7 9

Birth Number: Twelve
Musical Key: G# / Ab and Abm / F
Most Inharmonious Numbers: 1 6
Most Harmonious Numbers: 12 2 4 5 7 9 11
Relative Minor Numbers: 3 8 10

For more detailed information, go to numberharmonics.com

Epilogue

And now here is my secret, a very simple secret:
It is only with the heart that one can see rightly;
what is essential is invisible to the eye.

Antoine de Saint-Exupéry
"The Little Prince"

I have always cherished the St Exupery quote, "what is essential is invisible to the eye." You, as the Numerologist, can help others see the invisible and come to focus on what is the essential in their lives. But if you come to this with even a hint of feeling superior to another, or talking in a way as if you are better than someone, it really will turn around and bite you.

You are now at the close of the Practical Sessions. By now you will have an insight into the structure of Pythagorean Numerology, but structure is not form! For this study to take shape within you, a good deal of experience must be had. Experience is the only true teacher, and this book is merely a pointer for you to work with.

By now I am sure you understand that Numerology is not a religion, faith, or a path of knowledge. It is really a Path of Perception. Reading a chart is all about how you see, and what you see. This is what determines how you shape your thoughts and words. Your perception is a sword that sculpts away the dross of confusion.

As you step into knowing Number more fully, you will have some extraordinary experiences. It is to be hoped you will achieve what the Ancient Egyptians called the <u>Intelligence of the Heart.</u>

Retumburra is the Vedic word for this, and if you can discover this state within, the depth and breadth of your personal vision will expand to a degree that will surprise you.

Numerology is not a moral teaching, nor is it an immoral teaching. It is simply a way of seeing the world. However, this teaching does have a creed: *Let the past go, allow the dreams of the future to fade, and discover how you will become the eternal NOW* .

Book of Number: Practical

Number is impersonal, and in dealing with clients, it is best if you are as well. We align an individual's numerical facts to Aspects and Patterns that have specific meaning. In doing so, a date of birth and a name become a doorway to understanding, one that will show you how every person is full of potential. Only when we are as impersonal and detached as the numbers themselves, do we truly grasp this, and thus can more fully communicate our truth.

It can get a little crazy, where you can get so detached that a group of people will become a fascinating collection of cycles that mean specific things. This is known as being "In State". You float completely free of human connections, and it is truly remarkable how insights will flow through you. I have had this many times.

I used to go to a lot of parties and gatherings. People would ask questions, and I would find myself giving answers where the people would say in amazement, "How do you know all this?" You really can be the hit of the party and the talk of the town.

Of course, when you leave they will stab you in the back, because NOBODY likes someone looking better than they do at a party!

It can also scare people a little, that someone can, apparently, so easily see through the masks and walls they erect. No one likes to feel they are naked before the world.

So take care with how you give out what you know. Yes, you may have an extraordinary insight into a person's life, but remain aware as you speak that you can also inspire jealousy in people's hearts. You are becoming a channel for powerful forces. This can disturb people close to you, so be sensitive to the feelings of loved ones.

Absolutely no one is "better" than anyone else. We can be better trained and more experienced, and more capable, but there is nothing I have learned that another could not learn. And yet, the fact you have learned does mean you can have a greater insight and understanding of another's life and circumstances.

Life is an open book for anyone who knows how to read the pages. It is the Giving Tree to all, and everything we could ever want or dream for. But Life requires a payment: focus, application, attention, an attitude of goodwill, and an appreciation of the moment. If you have these, the door to Life's blessing is open to you.

A warning: I have seen good students delude themselves. So many have studied the system I have shown you in this book, and they get all puffed up when they realize they have what is called the "second sight". They become what are known as Mini-Masters.

The difference between the quiet achiever and the Mini-Master is usually to be found in the way they handle compliments.

People will be amazed at what the patterns of Number will provide, and they will say "this is amazing, etc." but I know it is really just an ancient wisdom I have learned to apply. It doesn't belong to me.

I generally defer such compliments with words to the effect "Really the compliment is for yourself, because a lot of people hear the words, but they don't understand the meaning. All I have done is read the patterns in your Numbers. It's like reading a book. But to hear what your numbers mean, and be able to change your life, that is the real challenge".

When people say you are wonderful, again, defer to simplicity. I explain to them that it is a spiritual principle that all we see is ourselves, so if they are seeing good things in me this is because those same things are in THEIR hearts. Obviously, the same holds true if they see evil in you! (as some fundamentalist types will)

You would do well to continually look for inner guidance as you go through a reading, and as you go through life. Stop and ask your inner guidance questions like "What is necessary here?" "Is there a better way to express this truth?" "Is what I say KIND?"

Overall, we can ask ourselves what Love might do in any situation, and this tends to give us a fairly direct path through to that special moment of balance we call happiness.

If you keep a kind heart and a humble mind, you will find all of this works much better. A kind heart is always given guidance, and if you ask for help, Spirit WILL answer in some way. It matters not whether you call Spirit names like Jesus or Buddha, or even Fred! The words do not matter to Spirit, only the INTENT does.

A Kind Nature and a Pure Intent are like a clear bell, ringing brightly through the morass of confusion that surrounds most of us. Spirit will hear this call, and answer you with wisdom and truth.

As we come to understand and rest in that space where our heart is at ease, we find the heart itself is a compass that guides us through the weaving ways of our own being. Finally we come to the state of mind that Saint Paul spoke of in Corinthians: *"At first through the glass darkly, and then, face to face."*

As our personal colors begin to shine through the mud of our past conditioning, clarity takes hold and we begin to shine. We will then begin to see far more clearly the life potential and capabilities of others, and hopefully we will find the words to help guide them.

Your pure intention gives you a great strength. It becomes a light to permeate the darkness of your client's problems. Yet our task is not to change others, rather it is purely to help illuminate the path.

In the end we learn the value of the legal term "Res Ipso Loquitur". The thing that speaks for itself, or that which is obvious. You will find that as you cut to the chase and see what is obvious, all you will want to do is to help others see this as well.

I stress that our responsibility is not to change or alter our client, but to offer clarity and thus to offer options. Options mean choice, and no-one with choice can be a beggar to life. If someone feels empowered to CHOOSE, they will find the inner drive to take a step forward to making a better life.

In the meantime, it is not my responsibility to sort out their "mind stuff" or their emotional baggage. My job is to make a clear point in a way that will stick with them after they leave.

To create a stronger impression, here is a simple technique: As you speak to someone, focus on a point some 50 cm (1-2 feet) behind their head. Look right through them to this point behind the head, and speak to that point exactly what you have to say, slowly and clearly. The point WILL come across more strongly, and leave the client remembering things better.

So, are we ready to become Numerologists?

In the following Book of Interpretations there is an enormous bank of information for every single aspect we have so far learned how to discern. Now the task is to tune into and grasp the resonance inside the Aspects you discover in a person's chart, and adjust the interpretations to suit their environment. Inherent in this is an understanding of the Client Psychology, and you are urged to start a study of this book as soon as possible.

Trust that life has a resonance you can tune into. Each aspect in a chart has a resonance, and it modifies in accordance to any other aspect it is linked to. These aspects will stitch themselves into the fabric of understanding in exact accordance with how well you grasp the resonance of the chart.

And finally, a little simple advice. To understand something, ask questions and be curious. If you approach every chart with curiosity and every client as a puzzle, you will do well. Always remember to ask the client lots of questions. Ask what they want to know. Ask where they have been, where they are going, and as each Aspect comes up, ask them how they feel it relates to them.

Asking questions reveals the truth. People just want to be happy, and most of their wants and wishes boil down to simple things. When you nail down what a person really needs you will inevitably find the desire for something like a new car is really a desire for things like recognition, approval or acceptance. Remember this.

Next in your study is purchasing the Book of Interpretations, that details a meaning for every Aspect we have noted in this book. With this in hand, you can start to put into practice all the lessons of The Book of Number: Practical Course.

Closing Comments

You have taken the first step on the journey. Developing the ability to work out the Aspects in any given name or date means you can now look up the interpretations, and therefore start the process of becoming a Pythagorean Numerologist.

You will need the Book of Number: Interpretations, and it is highly recommended that you also get the Book of Number: Client Psychology. This last book has many clues and hints on how to conduct a reading, and was originally an integral part to the correspondence course from where these books have derived.

As you get practised in this ancient art, you will discover how so many things come down to simple, obvious choices a person can make. The task of the practitioner is to help people make clear choices and as part of this process, understand the likely results.

It can be extremely rewarding, both financially and spiritually.

Should you feel that Numerology is a thing you wish to pursue as a life choice, there is the option to undertake basic tests and qualify as a recognised Numerologist with the Pythagorean Guild.

Write to qrcaustralia@gmail.com for more information.

We will also have at the bookofnumber.com.au website a free download for people who have purchased this book, which is a book of actual charts compiled by the author.

Be Your Own Oracle!

Did you like the Book of Number?
Did you want to know the next step?

Yes, there's more! Go to
www.divinitydice.com.au

Discover the extraordinary books on Dice Divination by this author

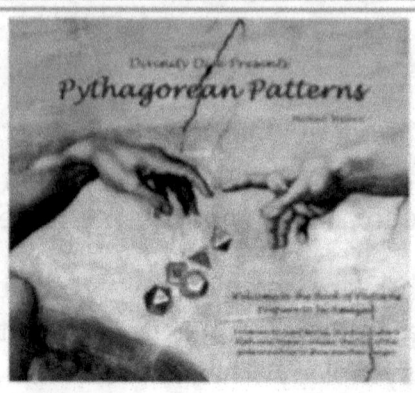

DIVINITY DICE

"Any one who is interested in Dice Divination MUST read this book"
                                                    Luke Rhinehart, The Diceman

Researched for over 30 years, the divinations given to you in this series are simply remarkable, both with their accuracy, and their layers of depth and meaning. Using knowledge that has laid dormant for 2500 years, Michael Wallace has brought to light the ways of the ancient Pythagoreans in a simple, easy to understand series of games.

Fascinating, and extraordinarily accurate, the Divinity Dice series is something right out of the box. Want to know more? Go to:

WWW.DIVINITYDICE.COM.AU

COPYRIGHT 2014

This book is published under the Berne Convention. All rights are reserved. Apart from any fair dealing for the purpose of private study, research, criticism or review, as permitted under the Copyright Act, 1966, no part of this publication may be reproduced, stored in a retrieval system, or transmitted, in any form or by any means, electronic, electrical, chemical, mechanical, optical, photocopying, recording or otherwise, without the prior permission of the copyright holder.

Enquiries should be made to the publishers at this Email Address.
qrcaustralia@gmail.com

ISBN: 978-0-9756994-4-7
Copyright 2014 Michael Wallace
Publisher: Ladder to the Moon Productions

Web: www.bookofnumber.com.au

Michael Wallace (Raven)

Michael Wallace is a remarkable individual. He is a Master Musician, Master Body Worker, Master Numerologist, Dice Master, Recording Artist, Songwriter, and Publisher. On top of all this he is also a prolific writer with over 17 titles in print.

Known as "Raven", or what the Hopi describe as the Storm Bringer, he is a catalyst for change and renewal.

www.ingramcontent.com/pod-product-compliance
Lightning Source LLC
Chambersburg PA
CBHW070808230426
43665CB00017B/2533